# Improving Your Memory

Human Memory: Research and Theory
Psychology of Learning: Research and Theory

# Improving Your Memory

❋ ❋ ❋

*by* Laird S. Cermak

W·W·NORTON & COMPANY·INC·

NEW YORK

*First Edition*

❋ THE TEXT *of this book is set in Baskerville by the Variable Input Phototypesetter.
Composition, printing, and binding are by the Vail-Ballou Press, Inc.*

Library of Congress Cataloging in Publication Data
Cermak, Laird S
    Improving your memory.
    Includes index.
    1. Mnemonics.   I. Title.
BF385.C356   1975      153.1′4      75–22158

ISBN 0 393 01124 0

1 2 3 4 5 6 7 8 9

*This book is dedicated,*
*in fond memory,*
*to Bill*

# Contents

# Foreword

❊ Most books about memory have been written either by professional researchers interested in communicating their findings to other researchers or by individuals who have developed a "system" of memory. The problem with the first type of book is that it conveys a good deal of information about the structure of memory, but it rarely presents any hints on how to improve one's memory. That, of course, is the major concern of the average reader, who otherwise would not be reading a book about memory. Research-oriented books also tend to be so full of technical jargon that the average reader immediately feels at a disadvantage. The problem with the second type of book is that it usually presents someone's personal system for memorizing; one that took years to develop and to use. The average reader is not interested in a system that takes so long to learn but wants instead some advice that can immediately be applied to everyday use. Furthermore, many of these complicated systems turn out to have only a limited use even after they are mastered.

I wanted to write a book on improving your memory that did not fall into either of these categories. Being a researcher in the area of memory, I was naturally familiar with many of the principles that are used to improve people's memory in the laboratory. I felt that if these principles could be presented to people in nontechnical jargon, they could profit from applying them to their own experiences. I was delighted to find that many people were able to improve their memory after having me lecture on these principles, so I decided that this should be the format for my book. You do not have to learn a complex "system" in order to improve your memory. But if you have a general understanding of how memory works, along with a few clues on how to apply this to your own memorizing, you will be able to improve your memory immediately.

The only goal of this book will be the improvement of your memory. No claims will be made that you will remember everything you see or hear from the time you finish reading. That is totally unrealistic. We forget because we are fallible; we are not pieces of machinery or computers. However, we all have the potential to improve our memory dramatically. This book will point out certain ways in which people could improve their memory by knowing how it works and by applying this knowledge to their own experiences.

We shall begin with an introduction to the topics that will be covered and describing the way they are organized. Then we will take each part of memory, dissect it, and explain what is known about each aspect, how it can be improved, and how it fits into the total memory system. Also we will see how the improvement of each aspect of the memory process will help you to remember information common to your everyday experience. For instance, you will be shown how attention to each phase of the memorization process will help you to remember people's names; important numbers, such as dates or telephone numbers; lists of information, such as shopping lists; everyday information heard in conversation or read in newspapers and textbooks; or lecture information vital to your course work or job operations. So with the improvement of your memory as our immediate goal, let us turn to an overview of the various aspects of this memory process.

# Improving Your Memory

# one

# Overview

## SCANNING OUR MEMORY SYSTEMS

✳ ONE OF THE MOST frustrating things that can happen to any of us is not being able to remember something that we know we should be able to remember. Sometimes this involves nothing more serious than simply not being able to remember the name of an actor who played a particular title role in one of our favorite old-time TV shows. But at other times it can be of far greater importance, such as not being able to remember the answer to a question on a test or forgetting an important appointment or forgetting to forward important materials to a client or to your boss. In these instances not being able to remember is much more than a mild irritant, it can create serious repercussions. At these times we all become keenly aware of the shortcomings of our memory, and in most cases we blame whatever evil spirit it was that endowed us with such an inferior mechanism.

It is imperative that you realize right here at the beginning of this book that your fear is not a unique one. Nearly everybody imagines from time to time that his or her memory is not only imperfect but, for some reason, worse than everybody else's. We all get the feeling that we must have gotten a lemon when the memories were passed out. Actually we are all born with essentially the same potential to build memories, but very few of us succeed in achieving anywhere near this potential, and, in fact, probably no one ever reaches her or his full potential. We should regard our attempts to fulfill this potential as both a personal and a cultural task. It is up to educators and scientists to find techniques that can be used by all of us in improving our memory, and it is up to all of us who seek to improve our memory to study these techniques, utilize them, and teach them to our children and to others. The outlook for memory improvement has never been better than right now, because we are working in an area that is just beginning to reveal its secrets, and its potential appears to be almost limitless. Some of the knowledge that has been discovered about memory and how to improve it will be passed on to you in this book. The steps that researchers have taken toward understanding memory, its shortcomings, its potential, and its utilization will be presented. However, it will still be up to you to incorporate this knowledge into your own future attempts at memorizing. Some work will be involved in learning how to successfully utilize what is known about improving memory and before these methods can become automatic for you. If you are willing to put forth this little bit of effort, you should find that your memory will improve dramatically and that the rewards from this improvement will be highly gratifying.

Before you can begin to increase your ability to remember information, it is important that you have an understanding of the way that memory works. If you wanted to improve the performance of your automobile, you would begin by learning all you could about how it works in the first place. Once you knew how it works, you could begin to learn ways to improve its performance. Finally, you would seek ways to apply this new knowledge to your own car. This step-by-step procedure is one that you probably would follow in trying to improve performance of anything you own, and so it should be used in trying to improve your memory. First, you should become acquainted with what you already have and how it works, then you should study techniques that have improved others' memories, and finally you should find out which techniques work best for you. Let's begin then to investigate the characteristics of your memory system as it now operates. You may be surprised to discover that there is already more to your memory system than you realize even existed. Scientific investigations of memory and how it works have turned up the fact that each of us actually has three completely different types of memory. These memory systems are called immediate memory, short-term memory, and long-term memory. Each of these retains, and loses, information differently. In addition, the life span of information within each system varies. Consequently, each is used for different purposes and we must learn how to use each most effectively. Whenever something is to be remembered for a long time, it should be placed into long-term memory; if it is to be remembered for only a short period, it can go into short-term memory; if it is to be used immediately, immediate memory is where it belongs. How we get this information into these various memories and keep it there will be the major concern of this chapter; the techniques that can be used to increase the effectiveness of each of these systems will be the topic for the rest of this book.

Let us begin with immediate memory. Immediate memory is probably the least understood and the most frequently overlooked of all three memory systems. In fact, most people are not aware that they have an immediate memory system. Perhaps the best way to describe this system is to tell you that you use it to remember things just long enough to respond to them. A typist probably uses immediate memory most of the time because she or he looks at each word and remembers it only long enough to get it typed. If typists didn't remember if for this very short time, they would not be able to get it typed. A telephone operator has to remember a number only so long as it takes to dial it. If operators were to remember it longer, if they could not discard it right after using it, it would be only a very short time before they would begin to confuse one number with all the others. As you are reading this book you are using your immediate memory all the time. Each word that you read spends just enough time in your immediate memory for you to use that item to make the transition from one word or idea to the next. Many of the words you read are discarded immediately, but you had to remember them long enough to make sense out of what you were reading. At this point in this paragraph you probably understand what is being discussed and perhaps can even paraphrase the ideas thus far expressed. But can you go back in your memory and remember how many times the word *the* appeared in the paragraph, or the word *you,* or even the word *memory?* Probably you cannot, yet you must have remembered each for a short time after viewing it, or else by the end of each sentence you would have forgotten each word preceding the last one and would not be able to make sense out of the sentence. This ability to retain information just long enough to use it is the basic characteristic of immediate memory.

This type of memory also comes into play when you are listening to a conversation and someone says your name. Even though you have been discarding most of what you have been hearing, the sound of your name is usually important enough to you that you detect it has come into your immediate memory and so you attend to it. Probably you will turn toward the person who said your name in order to learn what else they have to say. If you had no immediate memory, you would forget that your name was spoken even before you responded to that call. It would be as if the words went right through you and you could not catch any of them to hang on to long enough to even decide what they meant. If we did not have this kind of memory, we probably would not have survived as a species, since we need to be able to discard information quickly to be ready for more important information.

The major problem with our immediate memory is that it is extremely limited. It has been shown both in the laboratory and in everyday situations that we can only respond to one thing at a time in our immediate memory, and the decay rate for items awaiting a response is unbelievably fast (on the order of one to two seconds). Furthermore, we are limited in the amount of information we can retain in this memory system (estimated at roughly two to four items). This means that when two or more sources of stimulation compete for our attention, information from one source may be retained long enough for us to make our response, but the unattended information may not. In fact, at any moment you can respond to only one source of stimulation. You may be able to switch your attention rapidly from something like a TV show to a magazine and follow both, but that is only because you can miss much of the TV show and still keep up. If both require constant attention, you won't be able to do both at once. For instance, you cannot switch attention from one novel to another and maintain two separate trains of thought. Nor can you listen to a lecture and to your neighbor both at once. One is going to be favored, the other is going to decay from immediate memory within a matter of seconds. The material that decays is lost forever and, as far as you may be concerned, it seems as if it was never in memory at all. But research has shown that it was briefly in immediate memory but decayed before the person could respond to it. This was demonstrated by putting a pair of stereo headphones on a person and playing two separate speeches to the person, one in each ear. In order to get a response to just one speech, the person was asked to repeat each word played into one ear as soon as he heard it. As a consequence, the person was able to remember the content of the speech he repeated but nothing at all of the other speech. Now it could be argued that it never got into memory at all, except for the fact that it was also discovered that if the person's name were suddenly spoken into his unattended ear, he would hear it, or if the speaker's voice changed, he would notice it. So it must have been achieving immediate memory status, but decaying quickly and being lost forever.

As can be seen, attention is very important in determining what will or will not be responded to in immediate memory. Attention determines what gets plucked from immediate memory before it decays and gets lost forever. It also determines what to discard after it has been responded to and what to keep for further processing in memory for longer intervals of retention. This importance during the initial stages of memory makes attention one of the most important factors in determining how good a memory a person has. It is the first area that must be worked on by those who want to improve their memory, and some of the biggest improvements in memory can be seen to occur after attention is under a person's control. That is why attention will be the topic of the first chapter following this overview.

Our second memory system, short-term memory, comes into play after the information has been attended to and after information has been sorted out as being important to remember. Short-term memory is called a person's working memory because it is the system that is used to remember information that has to be recalled, or responded to, a few seconds or minutes after receiving it. For example, if you look up a telephone number, you have to be able to remember it long enough to get from the telephone book to the phone and then to dial it. You could not rely on immediate memory to retain this information, because it would decay before you got the number dialed. Short-term memory differs from immediate memory in that it allows us to remember several things at once (not just one) for a greater period of time (more than just one second). Nonetheless, it too is rather limited and subject to rapid information loss, though not as rapid as that found in immediate memory.

You may never have realized that you have a short-term memory independent of your two other memory systems, but this is the system most people use to remember information for brief periods. Nearly everyone realizes that it pays to keep saying something like a telephone number over and over to yourself in order to remember it. Consequently, we look up a number and then rehearse it until we get it dialed. We realize that the sequence of digits would probably just fade away if we did not rehearse it. What most people do not realize is the extent to which interference from other verbal information can also destroy our memory of that number. If you are asked to dial an unexpected number before the rehearsed number, you will forget the number. This might happen in cases where someone reminds you to "dial 1 before the number because it's not a local call." We also realize the devastating effects of interference on our short-term memory ability if someone calls out numbers at random while we are trying to remember a particular phone number. In the face of this opposition, short-term retention of the desired number becomes nearly impossible. As we will see, interference of this sort does not disrupt information in long-term memory (the next system to be explored) because this type of memory does not depend on continual rehearsal. You can easily remember your phone number no matter how hard someone tries to distract you by shouting out other numbers, because it is in permanent memory rather than temporary memory.

Unfortunately short-term memory is very limited in the number of items it can retain through its rehearsal process. For some inexplicable reason we are unable to rehearse more than *chunking* seven (give or take two) individual items of information. Everyone can remember strings of five, six, or even seven numbers in a row when someone reads them off (try it!), but most people are unable, even with practice, to remember eight or nine numbers in a row. Seven just seems to be our upper limit. Therefore, you should not try to keep more than seven items in short-term memory at any one time because you will overload it. Overloading can cause us to forget "everything" that was in short-term memory at the time it became overloaded, because it tends to disrupt the rehearsal process much the same way that the addition of a number prior to dialing the telephone interferes with our ability to remember that number. So keep in mind that you should never try to rehearse more than seven items in short-term memory at one time.

Fortunately, there are ways to overcome this severe limitation on our short-term memory. Some of the best ways involve techniques that will be described in detail in chapters 3 and 4. Basically these techniques rely upon an ability we call chunking, which is a process in which several items that we want to remember are grouped together in short-term memory and then are rehearsed together as one block or chunk. By chunking items, our short-term memory limits can be exceeded because if we have seven chunks of information in short-term memory, each containing three individual items, then we would actually be retaining twenty-one individual items. For example, you may want to try to remember the following twelve items, which, as you now realize, exceeds your short-term memory capacity: rabbit, horse, cow, elm, maple, spruce, carrot, pea, turnip, desk, chair, bed. You probably realized as you read that list that some of the words were animals, some were trees, some were vegetables, and some were types of furniture. Now in order to rehearse all twelve words until such time as you asked to recall them, you should group them into their particular categories and rehearse the category names: animals, trees, vegetables, furniture, instead of the individual items. This would give you only four items to rehearse, which is well within the limits of your short-term memory capacity. When it comes time for you to remember the actual items, you will find that if you recall each category name, the items under that category will also come to mind. If you have any doubts that this works, simply try right now to remember the animals, trees, vegetables, and furniture that were listed above (without going back and looking, of course). Chances are you remembered at least eight of the twelve items. If you did, then you remembered more than you would have had you been rehearsing each item separately (and you were not even rehearsing the category names, were you?).

Much more will be said about these methods of expanding your short-term memory in several later chapters. But for now, we will discuss the characteristics, limitations, and potential of your long-term memory. We can define long-term memory as memory for information we heard or saw minutes, hours, days, weeks, or even years before we had to remember it. Obviously it is retention of information that we have not been rehearsing continuously since the first time we saw it. Instead it is memory for information that we learned a long time ago and only now want to use. Since the information is no longer in our short-term rehearsal system, we have to search for it in long-term memory. The ease with which we search depends in large part upon the way in which our collection of memories is organized. Techniques that can be used to organize our long-term memory will be described in later chapters on organization, imagery, and mnemonics. But, for now, it is important for us to realize that the way in which we initially organize information coming into long-term memory is more important to its eventual retrieval than anything we can do at the actual time of retrieval.

Trying to retrieve an object that you did not put in its proper place is never more frustrating than when you are searching for a personal possession such as a ring. For some reason you may have put it somewhere other than its usual location and now you cannot remember where. There is nothing that you can do now to find the ring that comes close to how easy it would have been to put it in the correct location in the first place. This is true of your long-term memory as well. The major reason we have difficulty remembering things we learned days or weeks ago is that we did not organize what we learned into memory in such a way that we could find it easily in the future. Throughout this book we shall be emphasizing that memory is improved primarily by improving your organization of information, rather than by increasing your capacity to store information.

Actually we all have more capacity to store information in long-term memory than we will ever need or use. Unlike short-term memory, long-term memory is not limited in the number of items it can retain. No one can exceed the limits of long-term memory because it is limitless. It is how we organize things in this giant cavern that determines whether or not we can retrieve them. In fact, it is believed that the more information there is in long-term memory, the easier, not harder, it is to get more information in; because the more you know, the more complete your organization system must be and the faster you can catalogue new information. Whenever you have to make a new file for completely new information, it takes time. If there is already a place for it, it can be done rapidly. So not only does a well-organized long-term memory facilitate retrieval, it also facilitates learning and memorizing new material. Organization is the key to improved long-term memory and will be stressed over and over in this book.

The three memory systems that we have just described do not actually operate totally independently of one another. Long-term memory is dependent upon short-term memory because it takes time to organize new material into the system, and much would be lost before it ever got organized if we were not able to rehearse it over and over while trying to determine how best to file it away. Since short-term memory is so limited, we want to be certain that we are not rehearsing irrelevant or inconsequential information at the expense of more important information. Thus, short-term memory is in turn dependent upon immediate memory to be able to sift out what is important to rehearse from what is not. Also the three must cooperate during the process of chunking, because this involves detecting categories, rehearsing those categories, and then organizing the material into long-term memory on the basis of these categories.

It may be helpful in understanding how these three systems depend upon one another to follow some item of information through the three systems. As we wander about in our little worlds we are constantly being bombarded with information from many sources. We see things, hear things, feel and think things all simultaneously. Almost never, except when we sleep, are our senses quiet. We are always collecting information. All of this information passes through our immediate memory system but most of it fades away in less than a second and is lost forever. However, information that interests us becomes the focus of our attention and comes up for further contemplation. It is this information that we watch as it passes through our immediate memory, and whenever a particular item that we want to remember appears, we snatch it for further analysis. At this point it is placed into our short-term memory, where we recirculate it until we decide either to use it and discard it or to try to store it for long-term memory. Its length of residence in short-term memory depends upon how fast we can respond to it or how long it takes us to make enough sense out of it to organize it into long-term memory. Some information makes sense almost immediately, so it can go right into long-term memory. But some takes time before it can be understood and well integrated into what we already know, so it must remain circulating in short-term memory longer. Of course, as long as something is in short-term memory, it stands the danger of being interfered with and lost. Furthermore, no new information can get into short-term memory while it is full; and much may be missed as you are trying to figure out how to transfer something from short- to long-term memory. This may happen to you at a lecture or speech. If you begin to "think about" something the speaker said, you miss what he says next. Since most of us are afraid of missing anything in the speech, we do not take the time to rehearse and organize anything we hear into our own memory. That is why it is so hard to remember what a person spoke about, except for one or two key points that he repeated (rehearsed for you), minutes after the speech. You have to organize material into long-term memory. Once an item attains long-term status, it is more or less permanently entrenched. The probability that it can be remembered in the future is determined by how well it was organized. The better it is organized, the easier it will be to recall it. Of course, it sometimes is necessary to reorganize facts because they can get buried and irretrievable over the years as other things get organized around and on top of them. It always amazes me what I find perfectly well organized at the bottom of my desk. As well organized as it is, I know I would never have found it had I been looking specifically for that item. Just too much had gone on top of it. So I reorganize the drawer and put the item in its "new" proper place, easily retrievable because it now fits my current organizational schema. Such reorganization sometimes becomes necessary in memory too, as we shall see later.

Let's take another, more practical, example of how we can use what we already know about out three types of memory. Suppose someone tells us what to buy at our corner store. They may begin by saying, "We are out of milk, so get that." Our immediate memory should tell us that *milk* is the most important word that we heard and the rest is irrelevant, so we should put the word *milk* into our short-term memory. Next the person may say, "Also get soda and beer for the picnic." Now you have three items you are circulating—milk, soda, beer—in short-term memory. Next you are told to get three kinds of sandwich meat: salami, bologna, and liverwurst. Now you have six items in short-term memory. Since you realize that more is coming you start chunking these items under the categories: drinks and sandwich meats. The person then goes on: "Also get napkins, paper cups, and paper plates." So now you rehearse "paper supplies." And so the process continues. You decide what is relevant and rehearse it. If more than seven items must be rehearsed, you chunk it. Now let's say that you have the list just given: nine items, three chunks, and you say to yourself, "I won't be able to stop to get these until after work and I don't want to rehearse it all day, so I must find a way to organize it into my long-term memory." One of the many systems that will be suggested in later chapters (and one of the simplest) involves making a code word out of the first letters of each chunk you are rehearsing. The three chunks are: *d*rinks, (sandwich) *m*eats, and *p*aper supplies—*d, m,* and *p.* One word that comes to mind readily is DaMP. And, of course, you hope that the weather for your picnic is not "damp." Now all you have to remember when you leave work is the word *damp.* From that you reconstruct the categories: drinks, meats, and paper, and from that the items: milk, soda, beer, salami, bologna, liverwurst, napkins, paper cups, and paper plates. Sound complicated? Well, perhaps by the time you finish this book, it will become automatic.

Now that we have seen something of how the memory process operates, we can look at techniques to improve memory. Some of these you can apply immediately; others are going to take time and practice before they become automatic. These techniques will be introduced by first attacking the area of attention and immediate memory and improving your basic collecting of information. This will be the major objective of chapter 2, the chapter on attention. Then we will progress to those procedures for increasing the capabilities of your short-term memory system. You will discover in chapters 3 and 4 the methods for chunking information during rehearsal, namely organization and mediation. These also provide the first steps in the transference of that very material into your permanent long-term memory. Finally, those schemas that have been developed to enable rapid and effective organization of information in long-term memory will be explored. The first of these, mediation, relies upon the linking of new knowledge to old. The seond technique, imagery, relies upon your ability to mentally picture the information. This procedure, described in chapter 5, has been shown to be an extremely effective way to remember information, but it must be done correctly and takes some practice. Finally, we shall describe some methods of memorization called mnemonics. These are used by memory experts to remember vast amounts of information but you can also use them in retaining everyday information. These will be described in chapter 6. In chapter 7 we shall review all the principles we have learned.

Within each of these chapters specific examples will be given showing how to apply the principles discussed to the retention of names, numbers, lists of items, everyday information, and textbook material. Hints on how to apply the principles to other information will also be given from time to time, but the emphasis will always be upon you. The more often you try to apply these principles to situations that come up in your daily life, the more they will become second nature to you and the more automatically you will use them. Now you are ready to begin. Remember, be patient; practice and utilize what you learn; don't expect miracles overnight; and, above all, enjoy the process of learning to increase your memory power.

*two*

# Attention

## FOCUSING ON MATERIAL WE WANT
## IN OUR MEMORY

✳ A PREREQUISITE to an improvement in anyone's memory is an increased ability to pay attention to relevant information. We all realize that we miss an awful lot of information every time that we allow our attention to wander. You probably have had the experience of reading an entire page in a book and then remembering absolutely nothing of what you read. This occurs because you allow your attention to wander to other matters while your eyes continue to move forward along the page. As a consequence, you may have to read the same material over and over. The same thing may happen when you are driving along in a car and suddenly you realize that you can't remember much of the scenery for the last mile or so. You were not paying attention to the scene before you, and that is why you remember nothing about it. Or you may lose interest in what a lecturer, teacher, boss, parent, or spouse is saying and stare out of a window or at a wall. You miss what is being said to you, which can be embarrassing if you are suddenly asked to give your opinion about what is being discussed. We have all had many such experiences in which our wandering attention results in little information getting into our memory so we know how vital it is to improve our attentive abilities.

It must be emphasized that even in the above examples our

attention is never completely tuned out from everything; however, it gets diverted from one source of stimulation to another. Our attention is only turned off when we are asleep, but when we are awake, it is always on, though it is directed toward only one thing at a time. It probably operates a lot like the channel selector on a TV, in that we can only be watching one station at a time, so we miss what is going on simultaneously on the other stations. We may try to flip to another station to catch what is going on on both stations but at any one point we can be watching only one station. Our attention works precisely this way; we can attend to only one source of stimulation at a time. Since our attention is so limited, so narrow, we must use it wisely and tune it into the most important stimulus source around us at the time. If something very important is being said to you, it would be foolhardy to try to simultaneously follow a conversation in the next room, a program on TV, or the course of an ant's progression across the floor of the room you are in.

Every day many events, people, and stimuli compete for our attention, often simultaneously. Two factors act to determine which of these stimuli catch our attention. The better we understand these factors, the more control we can exert over them and consequently over our attention. The first factor involves the nature of the stimuli. Some stimuli can force themselves upon our attention because of their particular characteristics. Advertisers use these characteristics to get people to pay attention to their product so that buyers will remember it when they go shopping. Consequently, advertisers use bright colors, catchy phrases, loud noises, movement, or flashing lights in their displays; anything to catch your attention. Lecturers may change their voice patterns, use gestures, insert jokes into their lectures, or pause to break up monotonous patterns or to emphasize points. If they didn't do this, the chances would be good that they would lose their audience to other sources of stimulation. These advertisers and lecturers realize that what catches attention is any change from the usual. Novelty forces itself into our attention. Therefore, bright colors make the product stand out from the sur-

rounding drab world. Changes in voice patterns keep bringing
attention back to the speaker. Apparently, our attention adapts
to, gets used to, an unchanging source of stimulation and begins
to tune it out, but it always responds to novelty, to change.

The second factor that determines what an individual will attend to involves conscious decisions to attend or not to attend.
Since we are free to make this decision, our attention is not
"rigidly" directed by outside stimulation. We can choose to focus
our attention on particular aspects of our environment and can
effectively block out other stimuli or events that are competing
for our attention. Of course, this becomes progressively more
difficult as the characteristics of the object or event become more
and more attention demanding. For instance, it is difficult to
block out a loud, sudden noise like a gunshot. That will capture
our attention no matter how hard we may be concentrating on
something else. Nevertheless, most normal stimuli can be
blocked out by the conscious decision of the individual. This
may be done by focusing so completely on a task that all other
stimuli are not processed or it could mean something so simple
as getting up and closing a door when the noise outside becomes
so loud that it keeps attracting our attention.

While increased attention alone raises the probability that
something will be remembered, attention's primary job is to determine what information in your environment is important
enough to try to remember. This information is then selected
for further rehearsal, and eventually it is consolidated into long-
term memory. Thus, we have two components of attention that
we have to work on in order to improve our memory. First, we
must learn to better *focus* our attention and eliminate distracting
and irrelevant sources of stimulation, and second, we must increase our ability to *detect* the most important facts in any attended source of information. Everything from that source cannot, and need not, be rehearsed, so we must learn to choose only
the most important facts. We will learn how best to perform this
detection process after we discuss improved focusing of attention.

Simply focusing our attention on the material at hand represents one of the greatest difficulties we all have in trying to learn and retain new information. Basically this is because we are all afraid we are going to miss something else going on around us which might prove more interesting than the material we are trying to memorize. In order to overcome this, we must make the decision that, for the time being at least, the task at hand must be accomplished, and since you know you can only do one thing at a time, other pleasures must temporarily be forgone. It is best to set a time limit on yourself so that you will know precisely how much longer you are going to have to concentrate on one task before checking to see what else is going on around you. This time limit can act as a goad to keep going until it is time to reinforce yourself by allowing your attention to be directed elsewhere. If distracting stimuli are very intense (loud noises or voices, a great deal of movement about you, flashing lights, etc.), you may find it necessary to move to another place, where the distracting stimuli are less intense or absent entirely. If this is not possible, you may find you can block out distracting stimuli, at least noises, by listening to soft music through headphones while you are reading. Just make certain that the music itself is not distracting. But, no matter how you do it, it is possible that you can still be diverted from your primary source of stimulation. So any way you can find to avoid this will aid your concentration and increase your probability of learning the material quickly and easily.

Once you have focused your attention upon your task, you can turn to the second job that attention must perform for you—the determination of the most important aspects of the material you are trying to memorize. The important characteristics of the material depend upon what you are trying to learn, and they have to be delineated for each type of task. Attention must be trained to act like a filter, allowing some things into your memory system and discarding others as unnecessary or irrelevant. When we gain greater control over the attention mechanism, information can be processed more rapidly and we can learn to detect relevant information more effectively.

Concentration upon relevant information automatically increases its probability of being remembered. While the increase will not be nearly as dramatic as with some of the techniques introduced in future chapters, concentration must precede application of these principles and techniques.

We will now see how we might increase our ability to focus attention and detect relevance when trying to memorize names, numbers, lists, everyday information, and textbook material. In each chapter, we shall be applying the techniques presented to these five types of material. Other types of information can then be more easily assimilated because these five are similar to most other types of memorizable material.

### Names

Most of us find it much easier to remember faces than to remember names. This is because all we have to do to remember a face is to recognize that we have seen it before. In order to remember a name we have to recall a specific item without being given any clues at all. What we have to do ultimately is to try to attach a name to a face, using the face itself as a clue to the name. In order to accomplish this we have to learn to pay more attention to the individual features of a person's face, to the person's name, and to some connection between the two.

To memorize names and attach them to the correct faces, the first thing that we must learn to do is to look directly at a person, which, for whatever reasons, has tended to become more and more difficult in our depersonalized society. Some of us have even developed the notion that it is somewhat impolite to look directly at another's face. But these feelings must be overcome if we are going to improve our ability to remember people's names. You will discover that people actually appreciate it when you look directly at them while being introduced, because it shows you are paying attention to them and taking a real interest. The person to whom you are being introduced will respond to this increased attention by returning the glance and will begin to notice and attend to you as well. Good salespeople are well aware that a client will respond much more positively to a personal direct look than to an offhand glance followed by a look somewhere else. It shows that you care, that you are interested in the person, and that you are going to try to remember the name. So direct attention to the person's face serves two functions: It focuses your attention upon what you are going to try to remember and it draws the other's attention to you and increases the likelihood that you will be remembered, and remembered fondly.

Once you have focused your attention on the person's face, you can begin performing attention's second function of detecting relevant information. In this case you should seek those characteristics of the individual that set her or him apart from other people. These characteristics should not be traits like good-looking, poorly dressed, or tall. Instead they should be specific, such as a large, broken nose, or flaming red hair, or extremely bushy eyebrows, or a scar. Cartoonists are extremely adept at picking out those two or three characteristics of a person's face which best represent that person and they know that by emphasizing these features, the individual can be depicted by drawing only a small number of lines. If you can develop this ability, it will come in handy later on. Simply attempt to determine one or two features of the individual that will characterize her or him best and concentrate upon those features. Later chapters in this book will describe ways for you to memorize these features, but for now you should only be concerned with applying the two aspects of attention, that is, focusing and detecting the characteristic features of the person whenever you meet someone new. The next problem you should tackle is learning to attend to the name of the person you are meeting.

Learning names is sometimes very difficult because we are not always given enough time to concentrate on the person's name when we first hear it. Attention takes time and attending to names takes considerably more time than does attending to faces. We may be able to attend to ten faces very rapidly during introductions at a party, but we cannot attend to names as rapidly. Unfortunately, our host or hostess is often in a hurry to get us to meet everyone, so introductions are so fast that we end up unable to focus our attention on any one name. Consequently, we lose all of them long before we ever have a chance to analyze the name for any features beyond the mere sound. In order to remedy this situation, you may have to ask the introducer to go slower, or, if that is impractical, as it may be at a large social gathering, you could approach people some time later in the party and say, "We were introduced so quickly that I really didn't have the chance to learn your name; mine's _____." Now you will have the chance to focus upon the person's name and try and detect its unique features.

In attempting to detect features of a name to use in memorizing it, there are three things to look for: 1) Is it an unusual or funny name? 2) Is it a common name? 3) Does the name fit, or not fit, the face as far as you are concerned? There are several other things that could be looked for and some of these will be presented in other chapters. But for now it is important that you learn to focus on the name (it will help if you repeat the name after you hear it, or use it in a sentence as soon as possible, such as "It's a pleasure to meet you, Mr. *Brown*"). This will begin to direct your attention and concentration toward the name. The third thing to look for (does the name fit the face?) will also start you in the direction of attaching the name to the face.

The last step in paying attention to people's names is determining which name goes with which face. Here again focus and detection are the important factors of attention. At a social gathering you may begin to attach faces and names by looking at someone standing across the room and trying to remember that person's name. If you can't recall, ask someone what it is and then focus on that name while at the same time looking at that person's face. Begin to look for ways in which the person's unique facial characteristics might remind you of his name. You may notice that indeed Mr. Fish has a puckered little mouth, Mr. Schwartz has a very black beard (*schwartz* = *black* in German), and so on. This will help you to begin attending to the pairing of the person's face and the name, though such attention may have to come well after initial introductions.

Almost nobody can attend to all three stages of name-face learning during the brief introductions that are usually given at social gatherings. At best you can attend closely to the faces. Later you can attend to those names you didn't have time to attend to originally. Don't feel badly about this, because everyone who cares about learning names has to do it. Finally, you can begin trying to pair names with faces. It will take time because attention takes time, and you have to attend in three different stages. But take your time; it will come easier as you practice and as you develop some more of the skills discussed in the next few chapters.

### *Numbers*

Attention to numbers is not nearly as difficult as it is to names and faces. Numbers are impersonal, so there is no reason why it should be difficult to focus on the number you want to learn. In addition, detection of aspects of the number necessary to memorize that number can become a matter of pure deduction. The most important steps in remembering numbers occur after the initial attention. Nevertheless, it is important to realize that before a number can be committed to memory, attention must be focused upon it. You must choose it from among other numbers as the number to be remembered, and you must make certain that you continue to focus upon it and not be distracted by other numbers. Then you can attend to and detect relationships within the number. For example, if the number is 369-2468, you can probably notice that the first three numbers count forward by threes and the last four by twos. Of course, not all numbers have these obvious relationships, but many do. Once you have focused upon a number, you should try to detect

any possible internal relationship. If you find any, you will discover that it can aid your retention of that number immensely.

Take a look at some of the following numbers: Focus on only
one at a time and see if you can detect any relationship between
the digits. Then, after you finish the last one, see if you can recall
what the numbers were. Some help in detecting the relationship
can be found in the next paragraph, but first try to do it yourself.

543-2109
426-4860
107-4159
342-5167

The first two were probably easy, but the final two may have
been a little difficult. The first starts with the number 5 and subtracts 1 from 5 to arrive at the next digit, 4, and so on. When 0
was reached, the trend just continued on to the 9 because that
digit follows the 0 on a telephone dial. The second number starts
with 4 and subtracts 2 to get the number 2. Then it takes the
next even number above 4 to get the digit 6, subtracts 2 from it
to get 4. Then it takes the next even number (above 6), subtracts
2 from it and so on. The third number starts a little differently
because the 1 and 0 are viewed as a 10, than 3 is subtracted to get
7; 3 more, and 3 more again to get 4 and 1. To finish off, the
number 4 is added to the 1 to get 5 and then 4 again to get 9.
The final number also used the digits in blocks of two. (Knowing
this, can you go back and determine the relationship before
being told?) If not, then just try subtracting 9 from 34; then 9
again, and again. Now that you know the four relationships, try
to recall the four telephone numbers. It works, doesn't it?

Of course, as we said above, not all numbers will have such
internal relationships. Some numbers require some form of imposed organization or must be remembered by using systems to
be described in following chapters. Nevertheless, initial attention to the number will increase its strength in memory and
enhance its chances of being recalled.

## *Lists*

Lists of items that you have to buy at the store, pick up around town, or remember for a test should be attended to in much the same manner as attention to people's names, except that we don't have to attach each item of the list to a face. Instead we need some way to remember the entire list, sometimes in a particular order. Instead of learning pairs, we are learning a series of items. Still, we must begin by focusing our attention upon *each* item of the list. We cannot afford to glance over any items because those will be the ones most likely to be forgotten.

As with names, once attention has been focused upon a particular item, we should try to detect the features of this item. However, the major difference between learning pairs and learning series is in this detection process. In learning pairs we tried to determine what was similar between the two members of the pair. In learning series we should try to find other items in the list similar to this one item. For instance, if we had to remember to buy salt, grapes, apples, corn, oranges, pepper, peas, carrots, and paprika, we might detect, through careful attending, that there are three vegetables, three fruits, and three condiments. This increases our recall because we have organized the list. Through further organization and imagery we may remember even more, but focusing and detection must come first.

When order is important, we must focus not only upon each item individually, but upon adjacent members as well. We must use a somewhat revised pair learning in which each item is analyzed relative to what came before it and what came after it. For example, in memorizing this list of states—New York, Pennsylvania, Ohio, Indiana, Illinois—you must detect the fact that each state name is bracketed by two states that border it moving from east to west across a map of the United States. This would help you remember not only the individual items in the list but their order as well.

The key to learning a list is to focus upon each item individually and attempt to detect its relationship to other items in the list or to adjacent items when order is important. This initial analysis is the first step in your process of organizing the material into your memory system.

## *Everyday Information*

Focusing attention is of even greater importance in the memorization of information that you commonly learn in the course of your day, and in the learning of textbook material, than it was for names, numbers, or lists of items. By everyday information we mean all those experiences that do not come under the categories of names-faces, dates, or lists. It could include everything from the latest gossip on the block or a new joke you hear at a party to international news reported in the newspaper or on TV. It can also include what we popularly call trivia, or a news analyst's opinion on a world crisis.

Nearly everyone has met someone who is a whiz at trivia, or who can remember the capital city of every country and state they've visited, or who remembers the featured star of every movie they've ever seen, or the batting average of each of the Boston Red Sox in 1967. One remembers such information because of prior interest. If people had no interest, they would probably not have remembered it because they wouldn't have focused their attention on it. Once one's interest in knowing about a topic has been established, attention to that area becomes rather automatic. Our ears perk up when we hear it mentioned, we begin to seek it out, we ask about it, and we build more and more interest as we learn more and more. This doesn't mean that you *can't* learn information in an area that you are not already interested in. You can, simply by focusing your attention on that topic. Each time you see it written about, or hear it talked about, you say to yourself, "Pay attention, this is it." At first this will be slow and cumbersome and you might miss a lot before you realize that the topic is under discussion. For example, you may want to learn about football so you can discuss the game intelligently with someone you like. On a particular occasion you may hear several people discussing the Rams' back-field, and it may suddenly dawn on you that this is football and not farming. However, as you get used to the lingo, it becomes easier and easier for you to detect when the topic is being discussed and when you should attend to it. The same is true for learning the names of soap opera stars and following their escapades. At first, you have to consciously attend to what is being discussed and you have to learn to detect when it is being discussed. Eventually though, you will have ways of knowing what is relevant and what is not, but this takes time. Once attention becomes automatic, memorization is easier. If you don't develop interest in the topic, attention will never become automatic, and, especially if you become bored with the topic, detection of what is being discussed may result in your turning your attention away from, rather than toward, the conversation.

Attention to everyday information exists on two levels: automatic, because of a pre-established interest, and conscious, where the interest is not as intense. Since the first is automatic, it need not be your primary concern. The second is more important to work on. In fact, working on raising your conscious attention will increase your overall attention, so that even those areas that are interesting to you will become more easily detected.

You may say, why bother to do this; if I'm not deeply interested in the topic, why expend energy attending to it? The answer to this is easy. Without learning about a topic you'll never know for certain whether or not it's worthwhile. Roosevelt Grier, former professional football player, is interested in needlepoint; psychologist Joyce Brothers in boxing, so who knows what might eventually strike your fancy. Where should you start? Start with a topic that interests your friend, roommate, spouse, or acquaintance. That gives you a resource from whom you can extract information. Then just start attending to everything you see, hear, or read about the topic. It may result in your becoming taken with it, or it may not. It may result in your taking a side route, picking up on a related topic, then one related to that, and so on until you are far from the original topic. The key point to remember is that conscious attention is needed before any learning can occur; automatic attention is activated only in the presence of interest.

### *Textbook Material*

Interest also plays a large role in determining what we will focus our attention on when learning from a textbook. However, there are two differences between this type of learning and learning everyday information. The first is how we focus our attention. It has been discovered that a great deal more concentration is needed to focus our attention on textbooks than to focus on everyday experiences unless the level of interest is extremely high. Consequently, our concentration must be improved before memorization from textbooks can be improved. The second difference between textbook learning and everyday information learning is that in a textbook, detection of relevant information is much more difficult. Determining what information is *most* important to memorize is very important in textbook learning, but we sometimes have to finish reading an entire paragraph, section, or even chapter before we know what is relevant.

To detect relevancy, first we must improve our concentration (which is merely a form of extended attention). We all tend to prefer novelty; we are easily attracted by it and sometimes even seek it out. Concentration on textbook information is *easily* disrupted for absolutely *everyone* by any novel stimulus. Therefore we must work on preventing the possibility that our concentration will be disrupted. This can be accomplished by finding a quiet place and avoiding visual distractions. If you find yourself constantly staring out the window (scenes on a street are constantly changing and, therefore, very attention demanding), simply face another direction or pull down the shade and block out those distractions. It is often difficult to eliminate all these distractions because we hate to miss anything interesting that may be happening. So remember what you should do. Block off a period of time (one to two hours) during which you are convinced that nothing too dramatic could possibly happen. Isolate yourself for this time and give yourself a reward at the end by taking a break. Then decide if you want to try for another block or not.

Now that your attention is focused, you must learn to build up your concentration. Psychologists have shown that it is often very difficult to immediately concentrate upon the task at hand, particularly when it is very difficult. They suggest that you warm up to your task by first reading simpler material. For example, you could read a magazine, a letter, or a novel for ten minutes before studying. This will aid your concentration immensely.

The next problem is the detection of what is relevant in the material; what material you want to scrutinize later. As we already pointed out, this may be difficult because you don't know what the whole chapter is about until you've finished it. You don't know whether something is important or not until you see it in the context of the whole chapter. So in studying a chapter you should first read the whole thing through once without trying to memorize anything. Don't get bogged down in details. Read for feel; get an idea of what the entire chapter is about. This will not only help you to see the parts in relation to the whole, but it will also further increase your concentration, since it is still relatively light reading at this point.

Now you are ready to pay greater attention to the details of the chapter. So, go back a second time and read the text more slowly and carefully. This time you should analyze each point the author makes in relation to the emphasis of the chapter as a whole. These points should be marked by checks, underscored, or highlighted by whatever technique you prefer. Remember that you are looking for the most important points though, and not each detail. In many cases overzealous students highlight nearly every sentence in the chapter. This results in so much yellow that it draws attention to nothing, everything is the same. If you highlight everything, it shows that you did not pick out the *most* important points or ideas in the chapter. Instead you were lazy and inattentive, but wanted to appear busy, even though you had only yourself to fool. Educators have discovered that the better students in the class highlight far less in their text than do the students receiving the lower marks. The brighter students have highlighted just the most important points. You will find that it will make you concentrate more if you *limit* your highlighting than if you highlight a great deal. Concentration is what we are striving for, because *you* are doing the learning, your book isn't doing it for you. Besides aiding your concentration, highlighting will also help you to organize the material for further study, but we will leave organization for the next chapter.

In summary then, there are two important attention factors in studying textbook materials. First is the focusing of attention on the material, and second is concentration in identifying the most important ideas in the chapter. The next step (you're not done studying yet) will be to use what you have identified to aid your understanding of the topic you are studying.

As you can probably see, attention prepares you for the more cognitive aspects of the memorization process. It improves memory on its own, it is true, but the devices we have yet to introduce will increase it far more. But without attention, knowing ways to increase memory wouldn't do us any good at all. Always remember *memory begins with attention.*

*three*

# Organization

## PUTTING OUR MEMORY HOUSE IN ORDER

✳ THE SECOND prerequisite to improving your memory involves the development of better organizational skills. Organization is the key to easier retrieval of information from memory just as it is to the easy retrieval of items from a pocketbook, a briefcase, or a knapsack. People who simply cannot be bothered by organization end up spending more time looking for things they've misplaced than organizers spend returning each item to its proper place after every use. The same holds true for memorizing information. The person who organizes information as he learns it, who puts it into a proper niche in long-term memory, is more likely to locate that information when he wants it than is the person who doesn't take the time to organize as he learns. The first principle you should learn about organization in memory is that it takes time, but the time lost when you can't retrieve information when you want it is far greater. So anytime that you know you are going to want to remember something, or locate something, in the *future,* organize it in the *present. Take the time to organize.*

In order to organize incoming information it is sometimes necessary to use a pre-established system. For example, a librarian uses a highly efficient system for organizing a large number of books so that each can be readily located. Imagine what would happen if you wanted to locate a particular book in a library that had no organization at all. If the library had 120,000 books, you would have to go through all those books trying to find just the one you wanted. If, however, the library simply organized their books using an alphabetical system, location would be quite easy. But even this system is too simple for a library because sometimes people want a certain type of book, like a book on baking Indian breads, but don't know the author's name. In this case an alphabetical system by author would not help because the name of an author of this sort of book isn't known. So the library has developed a system of organizing books by topic and by author. *Incoming* books can fit immediately into the system. It is much as if the place for the book existed even before the book arrived. The development of similar organizational systems would be quite useful in improving memory as well.

The most primitive system of organization is "chunking" information as it comes in. It is impossible to remember more than seven numbers in a row by rote unless you group these numbers into "chunks." You can prove this to yourself by the following experiment. Without trying to chunk in any way, scan the list of numbers below and then look away from the page and immediately try to recall them in order. Here are the numbers:

7, 4, 9, 5, 1, 6, 8, 3, 9

Quite likely you were unable to remember all nine numbers. This is not at all surprising because, as you already know, nine numbers exceed the capacity of your short-term memory. However, if you now chunk these numbers into three groups of three numbers each, you may discover that it becomes much easier to remember the numbers. To test this, try learning the numbers listed below. This time read them in groups of threes (the brackets will help you to do this) rather than one at a time. As soon as you finish, look away from the page and try to recall the numbers in those same groups of threes. Here is a new number for you to try this system on:

(358), (627), (149)

Probably you just discovered that chunking makes recall much easier than trying to remember by rote. Do you realize that you just remembered nine numbers in order, which, without chunking, would have exceeded your short-term memory capacity? The point is that now you really only had to remember *three* groups, each containing three numbers, rather than *nine* groups of one number each. Using the same chunking technique, look at the number below and try to see if you can now extend your short-term memory capacity even more. Remember, group by threes; here is the number:

(472), (695), (721), (586)

The type of chunking you've just learned to use, that is, chunking by grouping items on the basis of the order in which they occurred, is good for extending short-term memory capacity but actually does very little toward getting the information into your more permanent long-term memory. To prove this to yourself try, without looking back, to remember the nine digits you first learned using the chunking technique. Were you able to remember all nine or did you find you'd forgotten most, if not all, of them? The reason you've forgotten it by now is that chunking merely on the basis of order of presentation does not provide a very efficient organizational schema of material into permanent memory. Chunking takes very little participation on the part of the learner and it does not require that he think about the relationships within the material. Only those organizational systems that demand active participation by the learner during the organizational process eventually provide a route for information to get into long-term memory. Take, for instance, the following nine-digit number:

1, 9, 2, 8, 3, 7, 4, 6, 5

Did you immediately notice the systematic relationship inherent within this number (the number skips from the lowest single digit, 1, to the highest, 9, back to the second lowest, 2, up to the second highest, 8, and so on)? If you noticed this yourself, it shows both that you were actively participating in the organization of placing this item into your memory and that you remembered this hint from the preceding chapter. If you did not notice it yourself, at least now that it has been pointed out, you should be able to actively organize it into memory. Several pages from now you will be called upon to try to remember this number and the chances will be very good that you will be able to rattle it right off without any difficulty. You won't even have to rehearse it between now and when you are asked to recall it; in fact it would be a better test of the theory if you don't rehearse it, because you aren't supposed to have to rehearse information that is well organized into long-term memory.

At this point in the chapter you have been introduced to two principles of organization: the first is that short-term memory capacity can be increased by chunking incoming information in the order in which it comes in, and the second is that consolidation of information into long-term memory can be facilitated by organizing it on the basis of a principle inherent within the material itself, that is, the relationships of numbers or items to one another. There are two other ways of organizing information into your permanent memory. One is the use of either mediation, imagery, or mnemonics, which, since they are the topics for the next three chapters, will be only briefly outlined here. The second procedure is to quickly relate what you are presently learning to information you already have in memory. This latter technique emphasizes the notion of placing new learning *into* an organizational system that already exists. We shall return to this concept once we have examined mediation, imagery, and mnemonics.

The use of mediation, imagery, and especially, mnemonics differs somewhat from chunking in that each "imposes" a pre-established system of organization on the to-be-memorized information rather than allowing an examination of the characteristics of the information itself to determine the system of organization. The *exact* nature of the mediation or imagery does depend upon the type of material to be memorized but the system itself (i.e., the use of mediation, imagery, or mnemonics) is independent of the material. A mnemonic actually forces the material into an already existing framework of organization regardless of the exact nature of the material, but in mediation and in imagery the nature of the information is important. Let us now see how each of these techniques operates.

Mediation involves the creation of a link between items that you want to remember as belonging together. These items and their mediating link are then stored as a unit in long-term memory. For example, if for some reason you wanted to connect the word *birthday* with the word *Republican* in memory, you could try to link the two together through the mediating word *party*. Then when you had to remember what word was paired with *birthday,* you could say to yourself, "What does 'birthday' remind me of? Oh yes, 'birthday party' and another kind of party is 'Republican' party." If you had to remember that the word *base* is to be paired with the word *park,* you could remember "base (ball) park." Mediation and its application to everyday situations will be discussed in chapter 4. For now, it is important merely to realize that it is a system of organization into long-term memory that relies on forming links between words.

Imagery, on the other hand, involves forming mental pictures of items or events that you are trying to remember. Then it is these images that get organized into your long-term memory. For instance, if you wanted to use imagery to remember that the word *elephant* is to be paired with the word *flowers,* you could form a mental picture of an elephant carrying a bouquet of flowers in his trunk. Then during retrieval you would try to conjure up this image again to help you remember the pair. Before you finish reading this book you will have discovered that imagery is an *extremely* powerful form of organizing and retaining information. More about this topic can be found in chapter 5.

The final system for organizing material into long-term memory is mnemonics, which involves either creating a rhyme or story that contains the to-be-remembered facts or involves using a pre-established story, or artifical schema, to remember the information you are now learning. You may already have used examples of the first type of mnemonic to memorize the way to turn your clock when a time change rolled around:

> Spring ahead in the spring
> Fall back in the fall.

Or you may have memorized the number of days in each month by the poem:

> Thirty days hath September
> April, June, and November
> All the rest have thirty-one
> Except February, which has twenty-eight
>     and twenty-nine leap year.

Neither example represents good poetry, but each facilitated your learning and memorizing of these specific facts and each gave you a system of organization of the material into your long-term memory. Although these two mnemonics are common knowledge, someone, somewhere, had to create them. Thereafter, they were just picked up by others because they were so highly useful. However, you could create mnemonics of this sort on your own if you took the time. There are many more mnemonics that have been developed but further discussion of these must be left aside until chapter 6.

The other form of mnemonic involves the use of memory devices that we call schemas. These devices represent techniques that can be used to remember any type of information by a preset plan. They are the techniques used by the memory experts that you may have seen on TV and are highly specialized. Each must be discussed in detail and each will take some amount of preparation, work, and practice on your part before they can be fully understood and utilized. Discussion of these techniques will also appear in chapter 6. For now it is important merely that you realize that these schemas also represent avenues of organization into your long-term memory. Mastery of these techniques can come only after you learn about, and can use, meditation and imagery, so concentration on these two techniques must precede introduction of this second type of mnemonic.

(At this point it might prove interesting if you would try to remember the *last* nine-digit number that you were asked to organize on the basis of the relationships that were inherent within the number itself. Do you still remember the number? We hope you were able to do so. Now try to remember the nine-digit number that you learned just prior to the number you just recalled. Can you remember it? Probably not, since that number was not organized on the basis of the relationships inherent within the number itself. Instead it was organized on the basis of the order in which it occurred. It was chunked by threes, which is a good system for increasing short-term memory capacity but not for organizing information into long-term memory. Organization into long-term memory depends upon relating the material to things you already know on the basis of the characteristics inherent in the information itself. When this is not feasible, mediating links, imagery, or mnemonics can be used.)

The techniques that we have just discussed for organizing material into long-term memory are especially useful for material that does not bear much relationship to other information we know, for example, lists, numbers, and completely novel facts. However, most information we learn relates in one way or another to things we already know quite a bit about. In these cases, organization really boils down to placing our new information into an already existing framework so that later it can be easily located and retrieved. We have spent most of our life learning about various subjects, and all this information has been organized into a network of knowledge that permits us to  progress from remembering one bit of information about a subject to remembering another. If such organization did not exist, our memory would be a hodgepodge of unrelated events and we would have to search everything (spill out the whole purse) every time we wanted to remember information. Luckily it doesn't work that way; we organize information relative to other similar information.

To demonstrate to you that you have already been organizing your memory to some extent, try to see if you can remember your grade school teachers' names from the first through sixth grade. You are probably imagining yourself progressing through those grades, picturing teachers' faces or the classrooms in which you sat. After you name your first grade teacher, you then progress to the second grade teacher's name. As you can see, you don't have to sort through your relatives' names, baseball players' names, or movie stars' names, because they are organized into their own networks, which don't get searched when you are looking for teachers' names. If anything is likely to interfere with your recall of a particular teacher's name, it is another teacher's name, precisely because they are organized together.

Using this speeds up organization of new information because you don't have to create an entirely new system. It enhances the chances of retrieval because new items are stored along with links to old information that can provide clues during retrieval. This organization can only occur through active thinking on the part of the learner. You must constantly be thinking about what you already know about the information you are now receiving and how this new learning fits in. In other words, you must organize the new information in memory by "thinking" about how it should be organized. It might help if you constantly considered how you might put your new learning in context with what you already know if you had to write a paper on the topic. You don't actually have to put this organization on paper (though that is sometimes helpful), but you do have to think about how you might do it. Organization requires active participation by the learner in dredging up old memories and incorporating new material into a logical framework that contains both old and new learning.

As an example of this, let us suppose that you are learning new information about the Civil War. If you concentrate simply on memorizing the new material, the chances are very good that you would forget it in a short time. However, if you try to imagine how this new information fits into what you already know about the Civil War, the chances of remembering it are much greater. Now, during retrieval, you can think about all you know about the Civil War until you zero in on that particular episode.

Remember how much confusion existed surrounding the events that occurred in the Watergate episode. The reason for all that confusion was that the information came out in a helter-skelter fashion. Until it all came together, it was hard to see how one event related to another. Consequently, it was extremely hard to remember all the men's names and all the events that occurred in any sort of order. However, as more information became available, it became easier and easier to put the pieces together. Then the names and the events became much easier to recall and to relate to one another. New information could then be learned more readily because it fit in place, and this new information became easier and easier to remember. One could begin to see that if so-and-so worked for so-and-so, then he must have been involved in such-and-such an incident in the Watergate affair. Although the entire story never really became perfectly clear (to say the least), as the facts became better organized, more and more people understood and remembered what was going on in the case. Whereas, nearly everyone was in the dark at first.

Now that we have seen several ways to organize material, both novel and related, into both short- and long-term memory, let us see how organization helps in the learning and retention of specific types of material. You will discover that those topics for which attention was least important in the overall memorization are sometimes those for which organization is the most important.

## *Names*

In the process of learning and remembering people's names, organization is not quite as important as attention, but nevertheless does play a part. You have to be able to organize the name-face pairing into your existing system of names and faces, so that the next time the face appears, it won't elicit a name that would rightly be attached to another's face. Most of the systems of organizing names and faces into permanent memory use principles that are going to be discussed in the next three chapters. However, one technique of organization, called organization by context, will be discussed here. Almost every one of us has had the experience of recognizing someone as familiar without being able to tell when you had previously seen this person. Usually you are also unable to remember the person's name. At these times you might have thought, "If I could only remember where I've seen the person before, I know I'd remember the name." Well, if this has ever happened to you, you already know what is meant by contextual encoding. Another situation involving context occurs when you see your doctor or letter carrier somewhere other than the usual place you see them. When this happens, you are very likely not able to recognize them. The more aware you are that contextual organization is important to the memory of faces and names, the more you will be able to use it to your advantage.

When you first meet someone whom you want to be able to recognize in the future and whose name you want to remember, take special notice of the setting and try to organize it into your memory along with the person's face. For instance, if you meet someone at a ball game, pay attention to the fact that a baseball diamond, ball players, and fans are around. Then look at the person again, then at the park, then the person, and so on. Try to pair the two together in your memory. This will help you to recognize the person later. Not only will you be better able to remember where you saw the person, but you'll be surprised how often the name will also pop out as soon as you remember the context in which you first met.

Another way to organize names and faces in your memory is by category. Fitting each person into a category when you first meet will help you to remember names. For instance, by remembering that the person you just met is a sales clerk in a ladies' fashion store, not only will you have pictured her in context, but you will have cataloged her for future reference. Cataloging means that you will have to pay closer attention to the answer when you ask people what they do for a living. Listen to their answer because it will help you to define them, catalog them, and organize them into your long-term memory.

It also helps to chunk people who belong together. This will enable you to remember one person's name just by remembering one of the other names in the chunk. You probably learned the four names "Bob and Carol and Ted and Alice" as a chunk because of the movie of that title. Also when you hear the name Steve Lawrence you probably think immediately of Eydie Gorme because they are paired together as a chunk. We often remember both names of a married couple because they are remembered as a chunk. In the future you should actively try to chunk names together. If you have trouble remembering the names of the children of one of your relatives, try chunking them together and memorizing them along with the names of their parents. Don't try to remember each name individually. If you can remember the chunk, you'll probably be able to sort out the names you've remembered and give the correct one to each face. Don't be afraid to chunk names for fear of forgetting to whom they belong. Remembering the names and having to sort them out correctly is far better than not being able to remember the names at all.

### Numbers

You've already seen in this chapter how organization by chunking can help you to remember numbers, but a few of these points about number organization should be reiterated. Remember first that "chunking" by order is helpful if you want to remember a number for only a short period. In order to accomplish organization into permanent, long-term memory you must find a way to organize the number on the basis of its unique characteristics, not on the same basis that you could organize any old number.

Do you still remember the number that had internal organization earlier in this chapter? If not, does the reminder that it skipped back and forth from low to high to low to high bring it back? We hope it did. Whenever this sort of internal organization is detected, a basis for organization into long-term memory exists and retention of that number will be much easier.

Another way that numbers can be organized into long-term memory is to make words out of numbers. A complete system for doing this will be presented in the next chapter, but to whet your appetite for this technique, let's look at an example of how it works. Take the three-digit number 321. We transpose each number into a letter and then form a word out of the letters, taking them in the same order in which they appear in the number, using vowels as fillers between the letters. A 3 is an *m* because of the three downward points in an *m.* A 2 is an *n,* for the same reasoning, and a 1 is a *t,* which is a 1 crossed. Thus, 321 becomes *mnt.* When vowels are filled in, this could become MiNT or MeaNT or MouNT. Any word you make up in this situation will work for you because all you then have to do is to remember the word and transpose it back into the numbers when you want to recall it. But more on this must await introduction to the entire system of mediation by transposition which appears in the next chapter. For now it should be sufficient for you to practice organization of numbers by chunking and by detecting internal organization.

### *Lists*

In list learning, organization is absolutely essential. There are two ways that this can be done: organization by category or organization by logical progression. Let's take each of these and apply them to the learning of various types of lists. After that you should be able to apply these techniques of organization to any type of lists you might want to remember.

Organization by category is actually a form of chunking that relies upon the characteristics of the items in the list. In addition, when you use this form of organization you may often find it necessary to rearrange items rather than keep them in the order in which they were originally presented. It should be used whenever several items in your list belong to the same category. When this occurs, you should simply try to remember these items chunked together. Say you are going shopping for the list of items we attended to in the preceding chapter, namely: salt, grapes, apples, corn, oranges, pepper, peas, carrots, and paprika. Don't, whatever you do, try to remember them in that order. Instead reorganize them by category: grapes, apples, oranges; corn, peas, carrots; salt, pepper, paprika. Then all you really need to remember is three fruits, three vegetables, and three condiments.

When you have to remember to do particular tasks during the day, your memory can usually be aided by using categorization by chunking. Suppose that on a particular day you wanted to: fix a leaky faucet, go to pick up dry cleaning, buy a paper, scrub the kitchen floor, get a new belt, pick up the dog from the vet's, take garbage to the dump, buy a birthday present, and pick up a package at the post office. Since there are three separate categories of events here, each with three exemplars, you could chunk them in memory as follows: buy three things (paper, belt, present); pick up three things (dry cleaning, dog, and package); and do three jobs (leaky faucet, kitchen floor, and garbage). Having organized them in your mind this way, you can then do them in any order, but a logical progression, as will be described below, not only further helps you to remember but gets them finished faster as well.

Obviously, chunking a list of items you want to tell to someone is also a good idea. Maybe you want to tell your friend two things about the picnic Saturday, two things about sports, and two about an assignment. Whatever it is, you will be better able to remember it by chunking, and you will increase the chances that your friend will remember what you've told him since you've organized the information for him.

Organization by logical progression involves the planning of a route that will allow you to accomplish what you have on your list in an orderly, logical sequence. This technique works best for lists of things that you have to do during a day, but it can also be used for other types of lists as well. As an example of the use of this technique let's take the same shopping list we used above. Assuming that you know where things are in the store to which you are going, you can plan how you will go through that store, what aisles you will traverse and in what order, and where you will pick up each item. Visualize yourself starting in the front of the store and picking up grapes, apples, and oranges, which you know are always stored there, then proceed in your planning to the vegetable counter for corn, peas, and carrots, then to the back of the store for salt, pepper, and paprika. Now when you get to the store, you need only to reconstruct your planned route, which, we hope, was a logical way to proceed through your store. Then, when you get to the check-out you should have everything.

When you have to remember a list of things to do during the day, logical progression makes the most sense, so let's logically sequence the list of things to do that was presented earlier in this section. The first thing that you would plan to do would be to put the garbage in the trunk of your car. Then you could plan to go to the corner where you could pick up laundry and buy a paper at the stand. Next plan to go to the department store at the shopping center and get a belt and a birthday present. Next you could pick up the package from the post office on the way to the vet's (for the dog) since that is a little ways out of town. Luckily the dump is near the vet's so you could then get rid of your garbage (which may be getting a little rancid by then anyway) when you get your dog. Finally, you could plan to return home and fix the faucet so you can get water to scrub the floor. If you follow your route exactly as you planned, you will get everything done and won't forget anything.

Logical progression can also be used when you call someone on the phone and want to be sure to remember to discuss all the topics you have in mind to tell that person. You might begin by explaining what happened yesterday (personal and sports), then today, and then plans for Saturday. Or you could sequence it by telling him first things involving the two of you together, then you alone (your personal plans), and then extrapersonal plans and information (sports, etc.). As you see, chunking, categorizing, and logical progression can be used together. Often when they are, it adds to the probability that you will be able to remember your list of information.

### *Everyday Information*

The most important thing to realize when attempting to organize everyday information into memory is this information simply *must* be related to something you already know. For instance, if you just learn that Linda Blair is going to be in a new movie, you should immediately relate this to the fact that you already know that she was in *The Exorcist*. Then later if someone asks you, "Do you know who is starring in that new movie playing downtown?" You can reply, "Oh yes, it's the girl who was in *The Exorcist*—Linda Blair." That, in a nutshell, is the key to organizing all new information into long-term memory. You have to be able to relate it to something you already know. Not only does this force you to think about the information and try to understand it better, but it also makes you dredge up old information as well. This reattention to old information tends to strengthen the memory of that material as well as the new material. Thus, this principle will be the only one given here for you to practice in organizing new information into memory: *relate it to something you already know.*

It will also be helpful to relate new information to things you already know when somebody gives you directions for going somewhere. If the person tells you of some familiar place near where you want to go, you will be able to remember where the new place is located in relation to something you already know about. It also comes in handy when you are learning to build something new (relate it to things you've already built); when you are learning the new season's TV fare (relate it to last year's; for instance, what is now on where "Mannix" used to be); when discussing politics; when learning about a trade of personnel in sports; when discussing the merits of a new product; when learning from a textbook (the next section) or whatever, remember to relate it to what you already know.

## *Textbook Material*

While the same principle of organization discussed in the preceding section naturally applies to the learning and memorization of textbook material as well, there are several other steps that you can take when organizing this type of material. It was pointed out in the preceding chapter that attention to textbook material requires not only concentration, but detection of relevant information as well. At that time it was suggested that you first read through a chapter quickly to get a feel for what is in it. Then, the second time through, you should read more slowly, picking out, and perhaps highlighting, the important points in the chapter. Following this, you should try to organize the material so that you can really learn and memorize it. Many books on how to study suggest that you prepare a written outline of what is in the chapter so that you can later study from that outline. However, while this certainly forces you to organize the material, most students are turned off by the idea both because it seems to be a sterile, impersonal, boring task and because most people simply don't know how to make outlines. Instead of learning someone else's format on how to make outlines, you should develop a personal style of jotting down important points; one that you feel comfortable with and one that does not get you bogged down in details.

You could first go through the chapter picking out the important topics in the text and then use each of these topics as the heading on a different sheet of paper. Try to limit these to around five to seven major topics because you are going to have to remember these topics when quizzed on the chapter. There are two ways to determine what these topics should be. First, the author usually uses subheadings in bold print capital letters centered on a page when he is trying to tell his readers, "This is an important topic." Believe him and use these topics as your headings. The second way that you can choose headings is to look at what you've highlighted. If there seems to be a particular topic that you highlighted over and over as being important, use that as one of your topic headings.

Now go back and jot down as many facts about each topic as you can. Many of these you will have highlighted; many the author will put as sub-subheadings in darker print then the rest of the page, some will be in italics. Leave space between each of these facts so that you can jot down further notes some time later. Next look at what you've written down under each heading. Ask yourself whether or not you understand how each fact under the heading relates to the main topic. Also ask yourself how it relates to the other facts under the same heading. If you find that you are not absolutely certain about these relationships, you should go back to the book, find out how they relate, how they fit together, and write down what you discover in the line under that fact. Always bear in mind that if you don't know your facts and relationships at this point in your learning, it's perfectly all right because you can always check back in the book. Don't settle for anything short of complete understanding, since further understanding will not simply occur by magic. Some suggestions for speeding up this process will be made in the next three chapters, but for now it is important just to learn the system of organization. Keep checking and writing down points to help you understand how everything under a heading relates to that heading. If you don't do it now, it will be too late during a test to begin thinking about how one thing relates to another in the chapter.

Once you have finished organizing by topic area and have learned the related facts, try to imagine what questions you would ask someone if *you* were testing them on this chapter. You should jot these questions down and then try to answer them as if you were taking a test. This procedure will further help you to organize the very answers, based on the facts in the chapter, that may actually be needed for the test. Caution must be taken at this point not to try to guess *precisely* the questions that will be asked on the test. This might allow you to formulate marvelously complete answers to these precise questions, but the chances are that these questions won't be asked exactly as you anticipate and so your work may have been wasted at the expense of additional learning. Instead of doing this, ask yourself just as many questions as you can and jot down key information that you would like to include in an answer to that question. Don't try to get perfect sentences, elegant phrases, or be creative at this time. Just jot down thoughts and go on to more questions. In other words, cover the field, don't zero in on any one topic. You'll be amazed at how this procedure will make you flexible enough to answer almost any question, no matter how it is phrased, on an exam. Worry about how to word it during the exam; not before it. Go in with facts and the rest will fall into place. This goes for any kind of test: fill in the blanks, true-false, multiple choice, or essay. The more personal, yet general, organization you have accomplished, the more prepared you will be for any test.

You may have realized that no mention of rote has been made up to this point in the study of textbook material. This is because during organization no learning by rote is needed; the mere act of organizing the information increases the probability of understanding and remembering material. Naturally memorization of specific information (names, dates, formulas, definitions, etc.) will be needed for a test on textbook material, but the memorization of this sort of material, which will be discussed in upcoming chapters, does not depend on rote either.

By now you probably realize that organization aids your memory because it puts everything into its proper place, thus making the search for that information so much the easier. The primary function of organization is to provide a means for the optimal level of storing and retrieving of new information. An organized memory is a good memory and an organized memory requires planning and concentration. The way you organize information during the learning process directly determines whether or not you will be able to retrieve that information at some later time. Now that we have established this principle, let us explore ways in which we can more easily and effectively utilize it.

# four

# Mediation

## BRIDGING OUR MEMORY GAPS

❊ THIS CHAPTER will discuss the first of three techniques for organizing our information into long-term memory in a more orderly and efficient manner than can be accomplished by mere rote rehearsal. Each relies upon different strategies for making information meaningful to you, since the more personally meaningful that information is, the faster you will be able to incorporate it into long-term memory and the more likely it is that you will be able to remember it. In many instances material will not automatically be meaningful to you, so it will be up to you to make it so. Of course, teachers, well-written books, and good verbal instructions can help to make information meaningful, but in the final analysis only you will know when something is meaningful and when it is not. The three techniques we will be using to help make meaning out of even the most meaningless of materials will be mediation, imagery, and mnemonics. Mediation makes sense out of material by making real words, connections between words, or sentences out of the material. It provides a technique that will allow us to verbalize everything from numbers to lists of facts. The second technique makes pictures, mental images, out of the to-be-remembered material, and the third technique, mnemonics, either combines the above two or makes stories or poems out of the information to aid in its organization and storage.

The most common form of mediation, and one that has been

researched extensively, is one that involves the insertion of a word between two items that the person is trying to learn together. For instance, in the laboratory a person might be asked to try to learn that the word *soup* is paired with the word *letter*. The experimenter might point out to the person that an easy way to learn this pairing would be to remember a third word inserted between this pair. In this case the word could be *alphabet*. Thereafter, when the person sees the word *soup*, he would be reminded of "alphabet soup." Being reminded of the word *alphabet* should help him to remember the word *letter*, since the alphabet consists of letters. The person is being asked to make meaning out of the combination "soup-letter" by inserting the word *alphabet* into his learning in order to bridge the otherwise meaningless gap between *soup* and *letter*. So now he is remembering the three-word combination of "soup-(alphabet)-letter." Thus, this simple form of mediation uses words as a way to *bridge* meaningless gaps between items that you may want to learn to associate together. Any time that you are unable to remember that two things go together, you should try to build a mediating bridge between them.

Suppose that you are trying to remember that John is married to someone named Tillie. Here you have a combination that needs a bridge because the two names do not logically, or meaningfully, fit together on their own. One way that you could remember this combination would be to let the name "John" remind you of the word *bathroom*, which could then be associated with the word *tiles* (bathroom tiles). *Tiles* is close enough in sound that it should then help you to remember the name "Tillie." Thereafter, you will probably easily be able to remember the marital combination of John and Tillie.

The system of bridging through verbal mediation can be used any time two items that have to be associated with one another in your memory do not automatically share a meaningful (verbal) relationship with one another. It works even in instances where names and occupations or positions have to be remembered together. For instance, if you wanted to remember that the Democratic candidate for state representative from your area was a man named Miller, you could remember first that the Democratic party was originally the party of the workers, and a miller is certainly a hard worker. Thereafter you would remember the combination "Democratic-(worker)-Miller" whenever you wanted to remember the candidate's name. In almost every case, invention of such mediating words takes some individual creativity. Luckily though, no matter how ridiculous the mediation is, and no matter how meaningless it may seem to others, if it is meaningful to *you,* it will help you to remember the material. In fact, the more novel and bizarre the mediating link is, the better it seems to work. At this point try and remember who we said is married to John? See, even if you thought the example was silly, it's a good bet that you remembered the name "Tillie" and that you will remember it for a good while longer.

One problem with simple mediating links or bridges of this sort is that their usefulness is limited. Very little of what we have to learn and remember during the course of the day comes to us in such simple combinations. More frequently we are asked to remember either isolated single units like a name or a number or a fact, or else integrated series of units such as directions, textbook material, or lists of things to do. In each of these cases a different form of mediation, other than bridging, has to be used. Let us look first at those instances where single units of information must be remembered.

Probably the most frequently encountered single unit of information that you ever have to learn and remember is a person's name. Remember that when mediating within a single unit we are trying to make sense out of nonsense. Just for demonstration purposes let's take my name, the author of this text, and see if we can make sense out of a name that has essentially *no* meaning in the English language. One way that I always ask people to remember my name (which is Cermak) is to ask them to think of me as just plain "Mac." But then I tell them that, since I am a lecturer and the author of this text it would be appropriate, though by no means necessary, to call me "Sir." The combination of "Sir" and "Mac" just happens to be the phonetic way to pronounce the name "Cermak." Surprisingly enough, this technique, even though I have supplied it to the learner, has helped literally thousands of people to remember my name. If you could invent a similar mediator for your name and give it to people when you meet them ("Bill White—just remember a bird's bill is white," "Simpson—the son of a simpleton," "Clyde Hooper—clodhopper"), they will be much more likely to remember your name the next time you meet. As you can see, the mediator need not be just one word. The only principle that *must* be followed is that the mediator has to make meaning out of information that has no meaning. You should try not only to make sense out of your own name so that others can use your system, but you should also practice the technique on other people's names so that you can remember theirs. Practice will make it easier and easier for you to use this form of mediation quickly, more effectively, and to your best advantage in remembering isolated units of information.

More will be said about this type of mediation later in this chapter under the topic of learning numbers, and there a system for transposing numbers into meaningful words will be introduced. Aside from names and numbers, the learning of isolated facts probably is the only other example of single-unit information learning. We have to realize that single units don't necessarily have to be single words; they could be isolated ideas, concepts, or facts that have to be learned. For instance, the fact that the capital of Massachusetts is Boston could be remembered through mediation. You could make meaning out of it by remembering that "A mass is a boss ton." *Boss* may be a bit slang for some readers but at one time it was used in the youth vernacular to mean anything from large to important. The capital of Illinois, Springfield, can be remembered by mediating it as "It's awful to be ill in the spring." The capital of Colorado, Denver, can be retained by remembering that John *Denver* sings about Colorado. As can be seen, mediation sometimes uses a whole sentence just to make verbal sense out of one fact. But the point still remains, mediation's function is to make sense where no real meaning exists.

Now, let's take the case where a whole series of facts needs to be remembered. First let's explore instances in which order is relatively unimportant and then instances where it is. Usually the best thing to do when we have to remember a list of words is to try to make a sentence out of them. For example, if we are trying to remember a shopping list consisting of a turnip, spinach, celery, lettuce, tomato, and beets, it would be hard to organize them all under the heading "vegetables" and remember them that way, since they are all vegetables and there are so many of them. It would be better to try to remember them using a sentence such as:

Let us turn up tomorrow and beat them into the cellar
lettuce  turnip   tomato        beet              celery

until their heads spin.
spinach

It is not so important that the sentence conveys little or no information about the real word so long as it makes some sense to you. Now when you go to the store you need only to carry this one silly, but meaningful, sentence and then by deciphering it backward arrive at the vegetables that we used to formulate the sentence in the first place. You should thus be able to remember what you wanted to buy at the store.

Now let us look at some instances of how we can use mediation to learn lists of facts in which order is important. In these cases you can either construct a sentence using each word *in order* or you can construct mediating bridges from one word to the next. You have already seen how to form sentences, so let us go on to successive bridging. Let us suppose that we have to memorize the names of the presidents of the United States in order: Washington, Adams, Jefferson, Madison, Monroe. Everyone knows that Washington was our first president, so let's use that as the first name as well as the bridge to our second name. Since the name of the first man on earth was Adam we can remember the combination of Washington–(first)–Adam. Now we need a bridge between the names of Adams and Jefferson. We could decide that Adam probably had a "jiffy son." Furthermore, this jiffy son was also a "mad son" (Madison). Nevertheless, we know that a mad son can still "man row" boats (Monroe). So now we have Washington–(first)–Adam–(had a)–*jiffy son*–(also a)–mad son–(who could)–man row boats.

A similar, and in many respects, easier way to memorize multiple units of information is to take the first letters of each word in the list and make a word or words out of these letters by inserting vowels between them. Take the above list of presidents, for example. We know that we want to keep these in order, so we have to take each letter as it comes: *W*ashington, *A*dams, *J*efferson, *M*adison, *M*onroe. One rule to remember is that whenever a vowel is a letter that has to be remembered, try to follow it with a double consonant to indicate the vowel is important. This means that you will always have to separate double letters (such as the two *m*'s above) by a vowel or use one to end one word and the other to start the next. In some cases double letters cannot be thought of to form a word. When this happens simply make the vowel into a single word of its own. *A* becomes *a,* as in "Run *a* mile." *E* is *he* (*h* never should represent an item itself when you form the word *he*. *I* is, of course, *I* as in "Here *I* come." *O* is *Oh* (again *h* is redundant). *U* is *you*. If the separate words you form also happen to make sense together, so much the better, because it will help you to remember the words. What can be done above is WAll, JaM, MAss (John Quincy *A*dams was the sixth president). Now by remembering these three words you will be able to decipher the first letter of the names of the first six presidents in order and from that you should be able to reconstruct the whole name. As you can probably tell, this form of mediation (forming words from initial letters) is a far better, and more effective, method than bridging from word to word or even forming a sentence from words. However, you should use whichever method works best for you. So try each one on to see which fits.

Try right now to remember our shopping list from above. Did you remember the sentence we formed? "Let us turn up tomorrow and beat them into the cellar until their heads spin." If not, then maybe you could use the first-letter mediation system. The list we had was: turnip, spinach, celery, lettuce, tomato, and beets. The first letters are *t, s, c, l, t,* and *b.* We can use the letters in any order in forming our word or words, but remember that a double consonant means the vowel was important, so don't use the word *battle.* One suggestion could be "LeT'S BiTe iCe." See if that helps you to remember the list. If it works better for you, use that method instead of the others.

This concludes our general introduction to the topic of mediation. We have seen how it can be used to bridge associated items, how it can be used to make sense out of a single unit of information, and how mutliple units can be formed into sentences or their first letters into words. Whenever we can make this kind of meaning out of what we are learning, regardless of whether it is meaningful to others or not, we have gone one further step in improving the way in which we organize and remember information.

### *Names*

The most important point in the preceding section was that making meaning out of meaningless information will help you to remember that material. The reason is that meaningful information is easier to organize, and therefore easier to remember, than meaningless material. Mediation makes it much easier to remember names and, while we won't be too concerned with the attachment of names to faces in this section, remembering names will also help you to attach them to the proper faces.

The basic form of mediation for the memory of names is trying to make a word, or words, out of a seemingly meaningless name. You have already seen how the author of this book makes the words *Sir* and *Mac* out of his name in order to convert it to two real words. It's not important that the real words be spelled anything like the actual name, since we're not interested in learning how to spell people's name. It doesn't even matter if the sounds of the words you make up are not exactly the same as the actual name, just so long as the mediator you form reminds you of the person's name. That is all that really counts. For instance, you could transpose the name "Anderson" to "hand and son" or to "and her son, both of which slightly change the sound of the name but still bring it to mind.

Constantly keep in mind that you should be trying to make meaningful words out of people's names. This actually forces you to do two important things at once: First, it gives you a meaningful way to remember the person's name and provides a mediating link to that name when you try to remember it, and second, it forces you to think about that name. Both these factors will increase the probability that you will remember the name. It may seem a little like magic to you until you try it, but once you begin to make sense out of names this way, you will find your ability to remember names will go way up.

Of course, some funny and even embarrassing situations occasionally arise, such as the time this author called Mr. Otheause, "Mr. Outhouse." But these incidents can be minimized by avoiding the temptation to make up words that could be embarrassing if they slip out. Or you could just be very careful when using a potentially embarrassing mediator. Actually this type of mediator—the ludicrous, crude, funny, or unusual ones —can often be the best kinds to use, because they are the more vivid ones in your memory.

In order to give you a greater idea of how easily this system can be used with a variety of names, several examples are listed below. A word of caution should be added, though. These names are presented just as examples of how certain names could be transposed to real words. You should *not* memorize these examples because the system works much better if you yourself create the words. And, since only you know what is meaningful to you, you should try to form your own mediators even for these names we use as examples. Here, however, are some ways in which this author has remembered the names of several people he has known over the years:

| | |
|---|---|
| Aaron . . . . . . . . . . | Hair on |
| Anderson . . . . . . . . | And her son |
| Bernardinelli . . . . . | Bernard kneeling |
| Boucher . . . . . . . . | Bout churn |
| Chomentowski . . . . | Show men to ski |
| Clarence . . . . . . . . | Clear ants |
| Darrow . . . . . . . . . | Dare row |
| De Luca . . . . . . . . . | The lucky |
| Evangeline . . . . . . . | Even jello line |
| Forrester . . . . . . . . | Forest her |
| Gavallin . . . . . . . . . | Gravel on |
| Herzog . . . . . . . . . . | Her dog |

Make up some more of your own to complete this list. Don't just invent names, but form mediators for some of your friends or acquaintances.

### Numbers

The procedure for the mediation of numbers in memory is a two-step process. Basically it involves transposing each digit in the number into a predetermined letter and then combining the letters to form real words through the insertion of vowels between the letters. Thereafter, the number can be remembered simply by remembering the word, or words, into which it was transposed, and then translating these words back into the correct number. In this system numbers are never transposed into vowels. Consequently, the problem of indicating when a vowel is important is completely eliminated. (This problem was discussed in the section where we made words out of the first letters of a list of items.) Therefore, repeating digits can be used as double consonants when they occur.

The system that will be introduced here is one that has appeared in many, many books on memory, so it is really nothing new. But it is a system that has been used by many people, including memory experts, and has been demonstrated to be the best way to organize numbers into long-term memory. This represents the first system that we have described in this book, but, as you will see, it still takes active participation and creativity on your part to use the system to your own best advantage.

The whole system depends upon the translation of each digit into a corresponding letter or sound each time it appears. For instance, the number 1 is *always* translated as the letter *t* and a 6 becomes the sound shared by the letter combinations of *sh* or *ch*. These sounds are similar and so a 6 can become either of them when it is transposed as part of a word. We suggest that you glance through the following list of numbers and corresponding letters and then go directly to the description of how each combination might best be remembered. After you have read this description, return to the list and memorize it completely. It is important that you be able to transpose each number quickly and accurately. Once you feel you can do this, we shall practice on some actual numbers. But first, here is the list for you to scan.

$$1 = t$$
$$2 = n$$
$$3 = m$$
$$4 = r$$
$$5 = l$$
$$6 = \text{sh } or \text{ ch}$$
$$7 = \text{k, } hard \text{ c, } or \text{ } hard \text{ g}$$
$$8 = \text{f, v, } or \text{ ph}$$
$$9 = \text{p, b, } or \text{ d}$$
$$0 = \text{z } or \text{ s}$$

There are ways that will help you to remember each of these combinations, but you must still practice the pairings to master them. So, after reading through these suggestions, get someone to call out the digits until you can give the appropriate letter or sounds for each. The best way to remember that a 1 becomes a *t* is to just imagine yourself adding the crossbar to the 1, then it would be a *t*. A 2 can be remembered as an *n* because the *n* has *two* downward points. Likewise the 3 is an *m* because it has three downward points. A 4 ends in an *r* (fou*r*), A 5 is an *l* because the roman numeral L stands for a 50. A 6 is *sh* (I remember "shix" in order to remember *sh*). The similar sound *ch* can be substituted whenever *sh* doesn't fit into a word. A 7 turned upside down is a Ⱶ ; draw one more line on it and it becomes a Ꝃ which looks like a *k*. You can substitute similar sounds if *k* doesn't fit, such as a hard *c,* as in *core,* or hard *g,* as in *gore.* An 8 is an *f* because a hand-written fat *f* is similar to an 8 (ℓ). *V* or *ph* can substitute as sounds for the *f*. A 9 is a *p* or *b* or *d* because they look like nines. A 0 is a *z,* the first letter in *zero* or an *s,* as in *sore.* Now you have an easy way to mediate from each number to its corresponding letter with some letters even having possible substitute sounds. First learn each basic pair and then add on the substitute sounds when you've mastered the basic list. Learn 1 = t, 2 = n, 3 = m, 4 = r, 5 = l, 6 = sh, 7 = k, 8 = f, 9 = p, b, or d, and 0 = z. Substitutions will come easy once this list is mastered because they sound the same as the letters in the list. Don't go on to the next paragraph until you are certain you have mastered the list and the possible substitutions. The time you spend now will save you an infinite amount of time trying to memorize or remember numbers in the future.

Have you completely learned the list now? If so, we shall begin to apply it to the memorizing of numbers. We will give you a seven-digit number (the size of a telephone number), show you how to translate each digit into its corresponding letter, and then demonstrate how to make a word, or words, out of the number. These words will then provide us with a way to remember the entire number. The number we will use is:

5 4 2 7 0 1 4

The corresponding letters are:

l  r  n  f  s  t  r

which become:

LeaRN FaSTeR

Let's take another example of a telephone-length number:

2  5  4  0  8  3  0

which becomes:

n  l  r  s  v  m  z

Add vowels we get:

NaiLeR SaVe MaZe

While the words from the second example obviously make less sense than the preceding example, they do nonetheless convey meaning. In the chapter on mnemonics you will be told how to form a picture which combines the words you have created from the number. This mnemonic will further increase your ability to remember the number. You can try this technique now, but it is more important for you to practice transposing friends' phone numbers (or important dates or any other numbers) into the appropriate letters, then make words out of them and try to remember these words either by rote or by pictures. You can even do it with very long numbers. For instance:

3  3  4  7  2  9  7  3  0  2  9  8  2

becomes:

m  m  r  c  n  b  c  m  s  n  d  f  n

translated to:

MeMoRy CaN BeCoMe eaSy aND FuN

Notice that in the above instance *y* is used as a vowel filler. Also notice that two vowels can sometimes be used to bridge the gap between two consonants in forming a meaningful word. Here are some other numbers for you to try to transpose and make words out of. But, before you do, try to remember the first number that we made into words in this section of the chapter. We hope you could because the number was 5427014 and its transposition promised you that with this system you would LeaRN FaSTeR. With practice you will also be able to 433945274 (ReMeMBeR LoNGeR) as well.

Try these examples before going on to the next section:

$$3\ 8\ 4$$
$$1\ 9\ 5\ 6\ 4$$
$$5\ 8\ 0\ 8\ 4\ 2\ 0$$
$$9\ 7\ 1\ 1\ 5\ 3\ 3\ 4$$
$$8\ 5\ 2\ 9\ 7\ 0\ 1\ 4\ 3\ 7$$

### Lists

Two methods that can be used to mediate lists of items have already been mentioned in this chapter but they bear repeating here. We will also introduce a useful variation of the first technique, which you remember relied upon your ability to link one word in the list to another through the use of mediating word or words. What was not mentioned previously is that this can be done most effectively if you try to make a full sentence out of the words (and their mediators) in the list. Remember the way in which we provided mediating links for the first five presidents of the United States by inserting key words between each name: Washington—(first man)—Adams—(jiffy, son)—Jefferson—(mad, son)—Madison, and so on. It is even more effective to make a full sentence out of these names and their mediators. For example, we could remember that *Washington* was *a damn* fine president, but his *jiffy son* was *mad son* who *man*ned *row* boats across *a dam*. Since the sentence still corresponds to the order of the presidents, we remember not only the names but the correct order as well.

This same procedure can be used in the memorization of a shopping list. For example suppose you wanted to buy: corn, squash, turnips, celery, and peas. Since order is not important here, we are free to put the items in our sentence any way that proves easy and compact. (Remember, if order is important the items *must* go into the sentence in order.) We could form the sentence:

Please don't squash my salary check because

(peas)      (squash)   (celery)

I'll have to turn up the corners.

(turnip)     (corn)

Obviously the use of a sentence makes recall of the list so much the easier. So, if you can form a sentence out of the words you have to remember, do so. However, most people still find it easier to remember lists by forming a word, or words, from the first letters of each word instead of whole sentences from the words themselves. Order is again maintained by keeping the first letters in order when you are forming the words. Unordered lists allow you to form the words using the first letters in any order. Remember that vowels are inserted between the to-be-remembered first letters except where a vowel itself is a first letter and is, therefore, important to remember itself. This vowel can be indicated either by following it with a double consonant (so remember, don't use a double consonant unless the vowel before it is important) or by making a single word out of the letter itself: *A* is the word *a, e* is *he, i* is *I, o* is *oh,* and *u* is *you.*

With the above shopping list the first letters ( *c, s, t, c, p*) could be used to form the words CoST and CuP. Then we would only have to remember two words when we go to the store, *cost* (which is easy to remember in a store) and *cup* (which is easy to remember when cooking). Since both words are related to shopping and cooking, an extra dimension is added to your organization. This naturally further increases your chances of remembering what to buy at the store.

### *Everyday Information*

When you want to remember something you just heard from a friend or read in the paper or saw on TV, devise a plan of mediation. Ask yourself these questions: 1) Is it an isolated fact? If so, try to make a meaningful word out of it. 2) Is it an association? If so, make a mediating link for the associate or find a way to combine the two components of the associate into a single word. 3) Is it a list of things to remember? If so, use the mediating link, or the full-sentence technique, or the "words from first letters" technique. In any case, decide what procedure would be most applicable, then go ahead and use it. Let"s look at an example of several different instances of everyday information learning and see which approach would be best.

First, let's take the learning of an isolated fact such as "The *fork* goes on the *left* side of the dish." Since this is an isolated fact (as well as a type of association), you should try to make a meaningful word, or words, out of it. You could remember this fact by translating it into the name of the apparatus used to stack heavy crates in a warehouse: a "fork lift." This will help you to remember this simple fact and the next time that you set the table you will look at the fork, remember "fork lift," and know that the fork goes on the *left* side of the dish.

Another example of isolated fact recall involves the ability to remember appointments. Suppose you have an appointment at the dentist at two o'clock. The way you could remember this is to remember the word *nod*. Why *nod*? Because 2 equals *n* in our number system and the *d* is the first letter of *dentist*. After the dentist appointment you may have a four o'clock appointment with the barber, so now you have a 4 (which is an *r*) and a *b*, which combined could be a *rib*. Now by remembering *nod* and *rib* you have two appointments you shouldn't forget.

The second type of material that we have to learn day-to-day involves associations. In fact, even appointments are associations, since a time has to be associated with a particular place.

Many associations can be remembered the same way that we remember appointments, that is, by forming a single word out of the first letters of each member of the pair. Suppose you want to remember that Sam's wife's name is Pat. You could remember the word SiP, which would be especially good if Sam is a big drinker. Or, assuming that Sam likes to tell the same story over and over, you could remember he always uses the "SAMe PAT-ter."

You could remember that Kojak is played by Telly Savalas by remembering the word "KiTeS" or "KiTS." Another way to remember this, or any other, associate is to put the two words into a sentence or a phrase as, for example:

> Go Jack, tell Lee to save a lass.
> Kojak—Telly Savalas.

Finally, when we have lists of everyday information, we should use one of the methods used to memorize lists (mediating links, full sentences, or words from initial letters). One list that you are often called upon to remember is a list of directions such as: turn right at the first light, right at the Y-intersection, left at the third street, and we are the eighth house on the right. To remember these directions, form words out of the important letters of each directional step (only one word per step if possible and never combine steps into one word). *R*ight at *f*irst *l*ight = FLaRe (the *r*ight can come at beginning or end of the word). Second step in directions is *r*ight at Y = RaY. Left at third street (remember a 3 is an *m*) = LiMe. Finally, eighth house on right = FuR. The directions are: flare, ray, lime, fur. This may seem highly cumbersome at first, but with practice and usage it becomes almost automatic to form the mediating words and to decode them en route. It might also prove helpful to remember a sentence which contains the key directional words in their proper order. "The *flare* sent out a *ray* the color of *lime* and burnt the animal's *fur*." Ludicrous? Not at all, because it works! Try it next time you have to remember directions. If you can just take the *time* to devise the mediating words and sentence, you will remember the directions. And the time it takes will be far less than the time you'll lose if you forget the directions and get lost.

## Textbook Material

The use of mediation in learning and retaining textbook material follows the same principles we've already outlined, because a great deal of this type of learning involves the memorization of isolated facts, associated information, and lists of items (some ordered, some not). The only barrier to overcome is the stigma that has always been attached to the use of these forms of mediation in the memorization of textbook material. Nearly everyone immediately sees the value of using mediation when learning names, numbers, and everyday information, but there is a great tendency to balk at its application to schoolwork and to learning from a text. Teachers have always argued against its use on the premise that it is a superficial way to learn and that it is necessary to learn *only* the material and not any additional mediators. Perhaps they are averse to evoking the mediator that Washington was a damn fine president, but his jiffy son, etc., in memorizing the order of the presidents. Maybe they find it demeaning to their subject matter to remember it this way: To remember the word *calorie* as "call Lori" or to remember that the nineteenth amendment is the women's rights amendment by remembering it as the "top war" (19 = tp, woman's rights = wr). But these educators should realize that how something is memorized is not important so long as it is memorized. There is absolutely *no* way that someone could learn all the amendments and their appropriate numbers by rote because they we're not written in a logical fashion. So the learner has to organize the material somehow, and mediation can provide an excellent way to do so.

Don't be afraid to use mediation to learn isolated facts, associates (who invented what, who was first to do what, etc.), or lists of words and to use any or all the principles suggested in this chapter while doing it. Just always beware that you do not do so at the expense of understanding the material. For instance, you could memorize all the chemical elements in order, memorizing their symbols and the groupings of the elements, by using mediation. You could even use mediation to memorize formulas. But, when all this memorization is done, it is still vitally important that you also learn *why* certain combinations can or can't occur, why elements are grouped as they are, and so on. You will discover that because you have already memorized so much of the table of elements, the understanding of why these things occur will come much easier than if the table had not been memorized. Since you don't have to continually look back to see what the symbol Au represents, you can progress to deeper material much faster. So use mediation to your advantage in learning about chemistry, biology, mathematics, history, geography (how else could you memorize the principal product of each state, *and* remember it, except by mediation?), civics, and so on, but be certain you take the time to gain understanding from what you are memorizing to use these techniques as tools, not crutches.

It may surprise you to know that even professional men use mediation to memorize the most vital information. Ask your family doctor how he memorized the twelve cranial nerves and you will probably find that he used a form of mediation in which the first letters of each word in the list are used as the first letters of words in a meaningful sentence. (This method has not been fully described here in detail, but you could try it for other lists and see if it works for you). Through the years many medical students have remembered the twelve cranial nerves by remembering "On old Olympus' towering top a fat armed German viewed some hops." The first letters of each word are also the first letters of each cranial nerve: olfactory, optic, oculomotor, trochlear, trigeminal, abducens, facial, auditory vestibular, glossopharyngeal, vagus, spinal accessory, hypoglossal. Now go and impress your doctor, but be sure to ask him how he remembered them in order.

Many school children remember the names of the Great Lakes by remembering the word HOMES: *H*uron, *O*ntario, *Mi*chigan, *E*rie, *S*uperior. A few people make up hundreds of these mediators to memorize facts in school, but most of us never use them at all, perhaps because we are afraid that we will forget the mediator. But a good mediator is much easier to remember than the straight facts because the mediator has more intrinsic meaning. Remembering twelve cranial nerves in order is very hard because one name does not lead logically to the next. But once you remember "On old Olympus' . . ." the rest just pours right out and you can then use the first letters of each word in your sentence to aid your recall of the nerves.

Use mediation in learning textbook material after you have organized the information in the text on paper, as described in the preceding chapter. At this point you will be able to see isolated ideas, associates, and lists of items. Then you are going to have to sit down and memorize them. Once you reach this point, where memorization is necessary, begin to use what you know about mediation to help you tie it all together, make it meaningful, and retain it in the future.

Mediation provides you with a technique for the rapid memorization of facts because it makes seemingly unorganizable material meaningful and easily organized. It provides a framework for organization where none was readily available. One final note to this chapter has to be made though. Mediators, once formed, have to be practiced and rehearsed. You have to occasionally say to yourself: How did I mediate Joan's phone number? or How did I decide to remember the twelve cranial nerves? or What was the mediator for that man's name I met yesterday at work? If you don't rehearse these occasionally, you will forget them. But once you have constructed them, they take far less time to rehearse than rehearsal of the actual material; and their potential for long-term retention is also far greater than the probability of remembering information learned by rote. Unfortunately, just knowing about mediation and how it works does not improve your memory. You must practice using it; transposing numbers to letters, making words out of first letters, making sentences out of words, and so on, until it becomes automatic. Even then it takes time, but less than the time spent learning and relearning the same material.

# five

# Imagery

## MAKING PICTURES IN OUR MEMORY

✻ THE SECOND TECHNIQUE that can be used to organize material into long-term memory is imagery, the ability to imagine something. As an example of imagery, try to form a mental picture of an elephant riding a tricycle. Undoubtedly you are able to do this even though the image is implausible and certainly outside the realm of your actual experience. Nonetheless, you can form a mental image of that event and, for that matter, of any event so long as each object in the scene is a concrete, imagable object in its own right. So long as you can image each object in a scene, you can image the objects interacting. You could imagine a scene in which a swing is hanging from a tree; a boy is catching a football; a car is tumbling down a cliff; a spider is rowing a boat; or a ketchup bottle is hitting a home run. What you can't image is abstract information. For instance, can you form an image of a judge dealing out justice or a pencil defending its honor? While it's possible to image the judge or a pencil doing "something," it is difficult to image anything like "justice" or "honor" because they are abstract concepts. Thus, imagery works best for concrete objects and actions. Try imagining the following scenes and notice which come almost automatically, that is, which can be formed as you are reading the sentence itself. Also check which ones are difficult or impossible to form. You will probably discover that the easy ones contained only concrete objects and events while the hard ones included abstract concepts:

A young man photographing a girl
A man admired for his honesty
A lion stuck in a tuba
A table caught up in adversity
A hurricane lifting a house from its foundation
An auspicious place bubbling with admiration
A field mouse smoking a cigar
An elbow lost in reverie

Did you find that every other phrase was difficult to image? If so, notice that in each difficult case one or more abstract concepts or actions was present. It is important here at the outset to realize that concrete images will form sharper images and consequently will prove to be more valuable aids to memory than will images that attempt to include abstract objects or events. If the image is fuzzy, and you must determine exactly what the judge is doing by handing out justice, it will be infinitely more difficult several days later to remember what the judge was doing. Thus the first lesson about imagery is that the more concrete your image, the more likely it is that you will be able to remember it.

The second lesson is learning how to use this knowledge of imagery to aid your recall. Actually there are two kinds of imagery, direct imagery and indirect imagery. A third technique utilizes verbal mediation coupled with indirect imagery. This two-step procedure will be discussed in the next chapter. For now let us concentrate on our direct and indirect imagery.

Direct imagery involves trying to remember an item, or list of items, by directly imaging each item of information individually. There is no need to translate the information into an imagable form before imaging it, because the picture that you form is a direct copy of the actual to-be-remembered objects themselves. Naturally this requires that the items you are trying to remember are concrete objects or ideas and not abstractions.

You may already have had experience using direct imagery when you were first learning how to drive a car and were studying for your registry exam. At that time you were asked to memorize the shapes of all the highway signs. For instance, you were required to know that an octagonal sign always meant "stop." You probably memorized this fact by picturing an octagonal sign with the letters STOP printed across it, so that whenever you were asked what a sign this shape indicated, you could simply imagine the sign with STOP on it and say, "That's a stop sign." You probably never memorized the verbal paired-associate of "octagon sign—stop sign," but just formed the image of the sign.

Even now you probably use imagery to remember where the instruments are on the instrument panel of your automobile. Where, for example, is your ignition switch? Probably you remember this by imagining you are facing the panel of your car and then picturing precisely where you stick your key into your ignition. Can you picture your instrument panel and tell where the headlight switch is? What about the heater? Could you do any of this without forming an image of your car? Probably not, because the image is so powerful that you can't wipe it from memory. Anyway imagery is probably the only way that you have ever memorized your instrument panel, so it is the only way you could remember the answers to any questions about it. In fact, when you buy a new car you wouldn't want to have the instrument panel described to you verbally because that would be almost meaningless. Instead you would want to see it, so that later you could remember your image of it in order to compare it to other cars you may be considering buying.

You probably already use imagery without even realizing that you are using it to such an extent. Can you describe the layout of your house without envisioning it? Can you tell what objects are on your desk from memory without closing your eyes and trying to picture the top of your desk? Name your five favorite ties, or dresses. Didn't an image of each pop into your head as you named it? Maybe you even imagined yourself looking through your ties or dresses searching for your favorites. Who sat in front, or behind, you in the sixth grade? Do you find yourself searching for a scene of that room or a face of the person in front of you? Hardly anyone would try to remember an alphabetical list of everyone in the sixth grade in order to figure out who sat in front of her or him. Instead we all use imagery.

Imagery then is a powerful tool for organization of information in long-term memory, but we must learn to harness it so that it can be used more effectively. Perhaps the most important step in using direct imagery more effectively is quite simply to be aware of how useful it really is. You have just been shown how frequently it can be used. In the future you should try to pay more attention to forming strong images of whatever you want to remember. Awareness of imagery's importance and concentration upon forming these images will automatically increase imagery's effectiveness.

Indirect imagery requires a transposition of the to-be-remembered information into imageable objects or actions. Whenever you run up against information that simply cannot be imaged it does not convey a concrete impression, you have to transpose it into a form that is concrete and can be imaged. The simplest way to do this is to change it into a word that sounds like what you have to remember and that is also imageable. This is most directly applicable to the learning of names. Some names immediately evoke an image, for example, Baker, Weaver, Hunter, Deere, Foxx, Lamb, Banks, Drumme, Marsh, Money, Rhodes, and Butter. But Popowski, Goethe, Vaughan, Cermak, Bernardinelli, and the vast majority of names do not. For these names we have to image not the name itself but a concrete object that sounds like the name. In other words, use the system that was described in the preceding chapter, that of transforming names into meaningful words. However, in this instance the words we form must be concrete objects or actions because we are going to try to form images of these objects or actions in order to remember them. We may transpose the name Bernardinelli to a (St.) *Bernard kneeling*. Then we will form a picture of a St. Bernard kneeling down. You should try to form as detailed a picture as possible and concentrate on that image. Later we shall talk about attaching the name to the proper face through the use of imagery, but for now let's concentrate upon forming images from transposition of names. Popowski could be transposed to being a picture of your *pop* on *skis* crashing into a tree yelling *ow!* The more vivid, bizarre, and personal you can make the picture, the more likely you are to retain it. So make the pop in the picture be your own father and imagine a tremendous collision and screaming victim. Always remember when you are forming an image that vividness, detail, and personal involvement will add to the image and to your ability to retain it. Also, we will see later, bizarre, unusual images are remembered better than normal, mundane images. For instance, can you still remember what predicament the lion found himself in in an image you were asked to form at the beginning of this chapter? Since it was a rather bizarre image, you probably remembered that he was stuck in a tuba. People have been known to remember this example for years.

The indirect imagery of names need not stem from the transposition of a name into a similar-sounding concrete object or action, but might instead arise from a more complex analysis of the meaning of the name. For instance, I help people to remember my name using imagery by telling them to imagine a knight in full armor wearing a kilt. The knight represents "Sir" and the kilt the frequent Scottish name "Mac." Surprisingly almost everyone remembers my name by remembering a ridiculous-looking knight in a kilt. Try forming indirect images from the following names using either the technique of transposing the name into a concrete sound-alike, or by analyzing the parts of the name and deriving images from that analysis in the same manner just done for the name "Cermak":

> Harrington
> Chester
> Timberlake
> Fillmore
> Clifford

Silverman
Blumstein
Caddigan
Brookshire

Now that you have formed images for all these names, how many of them can you remember? Jot them down without looking back at the list. Once you have recalled all that you can, check back to see which ones (if any) you forgot. In these cases were the images among the least vivid and well-formed of the lot? If so, you will have to strive to form better images for these names in the future.

We shall now show how imagery can assist your recall of specific types of material. Unlike the preceding chapters, we shall begin with a discussion of list memorization before we discuss names or numbers, because list memorization uses the direct imagery method best. The others rely much more heavily upon indirect imagery. Regardless of the technique you choose to learn, keep foremost in your mind that detailed, vivid images will assist your retention to a far greater extent than vague, undetailed images, which are likely to fade or become distorted in memory and be of little use during recall.

## Lists

There are several ways that you could use imagery to learn a list, but the most frequently suggested way is direct imagery, with a little chunking thrown in if the list is quite long. In other words, if the list is short, you should try to form one image containing all of the items, but if it is long, you could make more than one image per list. Suppose that you want to remember a short list of items that you have to pick up at the corner grocery store: milk, oatmeal, sugar, and butter. You should form an image that contains all four items, such as a picture of a hot, steaming bowl of oatmeal swimming in milk with lots of sugar on it and some butter melting on top. Remember the more vividly you form this image the more likely you will be to remember it. Now when you get to the store, you just have to remember your image and then you can buy all the items contained in that image.

When the list is longer, you might want to form images of several meals. Some of these meals might be quite bizarre, but that is perfectly all right because bizarre images tend to remain quite stable and are easily recalled at a later time. As an example, suppose you have a shopping list consisting of: milk, carrots, peanut butter, potato chips, spinach, cider, roast beef, bread, and fish. It probably would be best to form at least two slices of bread and spread the peanut butter on them as the beginnings of an imaged sandwich. Then add a few slices of roast beef to your sandwich (it may taste awful but it makes a beautiful image—a peanut butter and roast beef sandwich) and finally add spinach (looks a little like lettuce) to your concoction. This had better be washed down with something a little strong, so picture a glass of cider next to your sandwich. Then for a saner imaginary meal you could have a large fish on a big plate with a carrot slice over each eye and potato chips where the scales should be (bizarre enough?) This can be washed down with milk. Now try to remember, from your images, precisely what ingredients made up your two imagined meals. Can you remember them both? Vividly? If not, then picture them again and think about what it would be like to eat these meals yourself. Later in this chapter you will be asked to try to reconstruct this shopping list from the images you are now forming.

Now let's make a list of several people who have to be invited to a particular meeting. You could remember the names by using direct imagery and envisioning each person already at this meeting. If the meeting is to be held at your house, form a picture of John and Sue sitting on your couch, Bill in the easy chair, Charlie and Anne on chairs brought in from the kitchen, and Diane where she always sits, on the floor. Later you will be able to remember who is supposed to come to the meeting by imagining this scene. Then you could call each, in order, by checking them off as you go around the room in your image. If someone can't come, take them out of your picture. If you can't reach someone, picture them raising their hand (waiting to be asked) in your picture. As you will see, this technique borders on the use of a mnemonic because you have used your house as an agent to organize your images, but in this case it was intended that the meeting actually be held in your house. If the picture of your house was used simply as a device to enable organization of a list of people, or objects, that you wanted to image together, then you would be using a mnemonic, which is an external source of organization that gets imposed upon the to-be-remembered information. These devices will be the topic of the next chapter.

When we discuss mnemonics we will explain how "ordered" lists might be imaged and retained in their proper sequence. For now we must practice picturing the object alone or combined into a picture with other to-be-remembered objects before attempting other more complicated forms of imagery. This first step in the use of imagery should be used as often as possible until it becomes almost second nature. Eventually you will find yourself using it whenever you have to remember any small list of concrete objects. But always remember that when you form these images, try to make them as bizarre as possible and conjure up the image occasionally between the time you form it and when you have to recall it. This will strengthen the image and increase your chances of having it available when you need it.

Now do you still remember what was in that shopping list; that one that took two images in order to remember? Can you remember all nine items? Before you look back, ask yourself also whether or not you can remember the list of four items that was presented just prior to the longer list. Now check back to see if you were right on either one. If you got both lists right, you are a good imager. If you got the longer, but not the shorter, that is perfectly normal because we formed bizarre images for the longer list, but a rather common (therefore easily forgotten) image for the first. If you missed both, you need practice using imagery; so practice. In fact, regardless of how many items you got right this time, practice will tremendously enhance your ability to use imagery. Lists are a good way to practice imagery because they are uncomplicated and direct. It is suggested that you practice this form of imagery for a while before progressing to indirect imagery and mnemonics. If you feel comfortable with direct imagery, then proceed to the next section, where some indirect imagery will be added to what we have just been practicing.

### *Names*

We have already discussed the use of indirect imagery to aid your memorization of names. First the name has to be transposed into a concrete word, or words, that are amenable to being imaged. Then you can image the words into which the person's name has been transposed.

Imagery can also help you to associate names to their proper faces. The trick is to somehow include the person's face, or a prominent feature of the person's face or body, into the image that you formed for the name. In essence, attaching a name to a face becomes a process of joining an indirect image with a direct image. We pointed out in the chapter on attention that the ability to detect unusual, prominent characteristics of a person's face would help you to remember that face the next time you saw it. Now we will ask you to use whatever feature you find characteristic of an individual's face as part of your image of that person's name.

Let's take an example of a man named Kuberski who happens to have a gold tooth and a large nose. His tooth looks copper and his nose looks like a ski slope. If you can image a copper ski slope that looks much like his nose, you will find that the next time you see him you will immediately think "copper-ski" and you will know you are right. You could also have formed an image of a man skiing down his nose on gold skis. That would work too because you have included this man's prominent feature in your image of his name. Make sure that the prominent feature you choose to image is the first one you noticed when you met the man, because that will probably be what you notice first when you meet again and will, we hope, immediately evoke your image of that man's name. Naturally this technique is not as applicable to every name as it was for our example. But any time you can form an image for a person's name, try to include the person's face, or a feature of his face, in your image. This is important because recognition of faces is far easier for all of us than the recollection of names. The reason for this is that remembering faces is really just a recognition task (have you ever seen this face before, yes or no?), while remembering names is a recall task with no cues provided at all. Since recognition of faces is so easy, the use of that face can provide a cue for remembering that person's name. So every time you image a name, try to place a part of the person's face into that image. Then the next time you see that face not only will you recognize it as familiar, but you will also recognize it as part of an image you formed to remember this person's name. You can then use this face to reconstruct the entire image and then from that the name that formed the basis of that image. If the face was not part of the image, then the image used to remember this person's name is itself difficult to recall, let alone the person's name.

To practice this technique, let's suppose that you were to meet some of the following people; how might you image their names in relation to their faces, given one of their characteristic features? If you met someone named Carey who had big ears, how would you image his face and name? You could emphasize the ears in your image to the point where they are so large that you could imagine him carrying something. If the person happens to be a butcher, imagine him carrying a side of beef by his two ears. Then you'll not only remember his name but his occupation as well. Remember to make it a large side of beef and very large ears because that will increase your chances of remembering the image.

If you met a woman named Everett, you could picture her climbing Mt. Everett and, if she is especially prominent in the bust, imagine Mt. Everett in that location. If the person's name is Knieval, imagine an evil-looking knife sticking through his head in place of that cowlick. Make it as gory and dramatic as possible and the next time you see him that image will come back. In fact as soon as his face appears you'll see that knife, and his name will pop into your head as well.

Many more examples could be given but the technique won't work unless you can make up the image and connect it to the face. It has been proven that self-made images are remembered far better than those provided by someone else. Remember also that when you form an image, exaggerate the image well beyond the boundaries of reality. If you image a person named Butters by imagining butter on that person's face, don't just put a little dab on his cheek, smear it all over his face, in his hair, down his neck, everywhere. Overexaggerate your image to make it vivid because that will help you to remember it much better. If you meet someone named Harry Walker and want to imagine a man with hairy legs walking along, then make him really hairy, like an ape or a Neanderthal man or even worse, and make him walk in a desert or somewhere other than a usual place. Or you could imagine him walking in a race where everyone else is running.

In summary then, the use of imagery in the retention of names and faces involves a joining together of a direct image of the person, or a distinctive feature of that person, and an indirect image formed from the person's name. The only other principle to remember is that the more bizarre you make the image, the more vivid it will remain in your memory, and the more likely you will be to remember it.

### Numbers

There is obviously no direct way to image a number. To prove this to yourself (if you don't already believe it), try forming an image of the following number; look at it for about ten seconds, then cover it up and try to recall it from the image that you have formed of that number.

9 4 7 2 8 6 3 0 5 1 8 2

If you did succeed in remembering the number, it was probably because you used a memory aid in addition to pure imagery. The vast majority of people would fail even an immediate memory test if they tried to remember numbers through the use of imagery.

Unfortunately, there is also no way to remember numbers by indirect imagery either, because numbers are not amenable to our system of transposing information into concrete objects or events. It you tried to image a 1 as looking like a stick, and an 8 looking like a fat lady, then composed a little scenario with all these objects in it, you would find the image as difficult to remember as the number itself. You would simply have too many images to remember individually. Also, order is important in a number and this type of imagery can't give you order.

Consequently, the *only* way that imagery could help you to remember a number is by a form of double transposition. Double transpositions involve imposing systems on the material and no longer really use the item itself to form the image, directly or indirectly. Therefore, it comes under the province of mnemonics, and a further discussion of imagery of numbers must wait until the next chapter. However, we will give you a glimpse of what is going to be done and to explain what is meant by a double transposition.

The first step will involve the use of the mediating technique we have already outlined. Each number will be given a corresponding letter. Then words (concrete objects, events, or actions) will be formed from these letters by adding vowels, as we did in the preceding chapter. Once these words are determined, an image that combines the words can be formed which will be used to mediate our retention of the number. If this all seems complicated, don't despair. The next chapter will spell it out in greater detail, giving several examples to make it much easier for you to use.

### *Everyday Information*

Without your even being aware of it, you are constantly forming images of events, people, items of information, and other tidbits. Most of these images are not very strong though, and consequently they are not much good to us in helping to remember information. However, when we are aware that a visual experience we are presently having corresponds to an image of a visual experience we had previously, we usually try to remember when the first experience occurred. For instance, you may see an actor in a movie on TV and say to yourself, "He used to be on a regular show on TV years ago. I recognize his face but I can't remember where I've seen him before." This happened to my wife once when she saw Vince Edwards starring in a cowboy movie. She was completely unable to remember what program that familiar face (and voice) used to be in until I told her to picture the man in a doctor's uniform instead of a cowboy outfit. Immediately the image of "Ben Casey" came back to her and she remembered where she had seen him before because now her image of the man was completed.

Incomplete imagery, sometimes referred to as nonvivid imagery, is a very common experience for all of us, and it probably accounts for those occasional feelings of having been in a certain place before, or having seen someone before but not knowing where, or even having done something before but not knowing when. What we have to work on is our initial formation of these images. When we learn something that we know we are going to want to remember in the future, we have to strengthen our image of that information by making it unique and vivid. Merely being aware that imagery can be a valuable aid to memory will help you to do this, but practice will make it automatic. Then, even casual images will begin to be strengthened through awareness, practice, and mastery of the use of imagery.

Imagery can also be useful when trying to remember rules or instructions. For instance, if you still have difficulty remembering that the fork goes on the left side of your plate (even though we have given you one technique for remembering this), just imagine a giant fork stuck into your wrist in the precise spot that you wear your wristwatch. If you wear your watch on your right wrist, then picture yourself with your watch on one wrist and the fork in the other. Remember, vividness and exaggeration count but the image must tie into something that comes naturally, such as the wrist on which you normally wear your watch. Otherwise you may forget which wrist the fork was stuck into when next you conjure up the image. But if it was stuck right into where the top of your watch is (if you wear it on the left), you will remember that as part of the image. Then the side the fork should be on becomes easy to remember.

Another instance in which imagery aids us in remembering everyday information is when we have to remember how to put back together something we have taken apart. We often forget how to put something back together because we usually try to remember it by forming an image that is a perfect reproduction of the intact object. You shouldn't try to image in that way; instead you should exaggerate your image. Imagine yourself inside the object. What is above you, below you, to the sides? How would you get out? Surprisingly, this procedure will help you to remember how the object is to be reassembled. If many steps are involved, you may need to form more than one image, and it need not involve having you inside the object, but it should involve exaggeration.

As you can see, imagery can be used in almost any situation if you simply take the time to notice the important aspects of information, to exaggerate these aspects, and to make your image vivid and personal. If you are trying to remember directions, imagine yourself driving and making the turns, and exaggerate the relevant information. If you are trying to remember what time you have an appointment with the dentist, imagine him being the "Mickey Mouse" of a watch and put his arms in the appropriate places for the time of the appointment.

One final note about imagery in relation to remembering everyday information should be mentioned: even though you may not have been aware of how much imagery can help you remember things, the men who create the ads on TV are. Their whole job is to provide an image for you so that the next time you go to the store you will see their product, it will evoke the desired image, and you will buy it. Consequently advertisers have their products dancing, singing, flying, being squeezed, floating through your body, knocking out Mr. Tooth Decay, making people happy, pretty, or rich, and so on. They package their product brightly to catch your attention, but they also want their package to evoke an image which will remind you that you've heard of this product, know it to be good (because they said so on TV), and so you buy it. Creating an image is the job of advertising agencies whether it be an image for a product, for a politician, or for a program. So if you want to improve your own memory, make it *your* job to create images and don't leave it to the ad people. You don't want their images running your memory anyway, do you?

### Textbook Material

Imagery can be used in memorizing textbook material, but most of it will be done in conjunction with a form of transposition that involves verbal mediation. This will be discussed in the mnemonics chapter. However, there are some ways in which imagery can benefit your retention of textbook material without any initial transpositions.

During the course of your studies you can imagine yourself being at the place you are studying about, or doing what you are studying, or otherwise involving yourself. Try to form images that include you in them. Suppose, for example, that you are studying the Battle of the Bulge. Try to imagine yourself as one of the fighting men eager to gain knowledge about what is happening. Really imagine yourself at the scene. Ask yourself why you are here. Ask the name of the commander of your forces, the man who may decide whether you advance or retreat, live or die. What is the enemy doing? Why was the decision made to advance the middle of the line and not the extremes? You've seen enough war movies on TV to get into this scene, so do it. Don't just sit reading words on a page, get into the action of the scene. Not only does this make it more interesting, but it provides images that will help you to remember when it comes time to take a test on the subject. The rest of the students read about the battle, but you were there. Try it a few times and see if it doesn't work for you. Get into the scene when the Declaration of Independence was signed (sign it under John Hancock's name, the big showoff). Be there at Gettysburg, at Selma with Martin Luther King, and in Cuba at the Bay of Pigs. Get into the action and make yourself part of your images.

The same can also be done for subjects that are a little more passive than history, but can be imaged. Suppose you have to learn that the major product of West Virginia is coal. You could imagine yourself as a coal miner in West Virginia. Imagine yourself picking cotton in Alabama, forging steel in Pittsburgh, picking oranges in California, corn in Iowa, and wheat in Kansas. Don't forget to get yourself into the picture (that makes it personal) and don't forget to make it vivid and exaggerated (that makes it stick).

Obviously, examples of every subject you may study cannot be given here, so it will be up to you to involve yourself in images that you form about the topics you study. Memorization of dates, lists of names, facts, and other additional information not directly amenable to imagery will be covered in the next chapter. For now it is important that you realize that learning from a textbook does not have to be by rote. Not only is that the worst way to learn, but it is also the most boring. The use of imagery enhances your ability to remember information and is infinitely more interesting. Above all else, it involves you in what you are learning, and that is the most important factor.

Now that we have learned how to use mediation and imagery, we are going to turn to the last of the methods of long-term memory organization, namely mnemonics. One type of mnemonic is actually a combination of mediation and imagery (hinted at several times during the course of the present chapter). So, before you start the next chapter, it is important that you spend some time practicing mediation and imagery. Review the principles that you have learned about these topics. Then proceed and learn how mnemonics can improve your memory even further.

# six

# Mnemonics

## USING TECHNIQUES TO AID OUR MEMORY

❆ Mnemonics represent the third and final way that information can be organized into long-term memory. Unlike mediation
and imagery, mnemonics seek to impose order on material that
you want to remember rather than seeking order within the material itself. Mnemonics use schemas or plans of organization
that have been devised and practiced even before the specific
material that you want to memorize has ever been seen. Sometimes mnemonics employ mediation or imagery and sometimes
even a combination of the two, but the mediating link or the
image does not directly follow from the material at hand. A
mnemonic is analgous to an organizer in a workshop, a pegboard upon which tools can be hung. You could put anything
you wanted to on this pegboard and it would help to organize
your tools because they would not be scattered all about the
room. A pegboard can be designed to organize anything that
happened to be lying around, it does not necessarily have to be
designed for specific tools to be put in specific places.

Actually, there are two different types of mnemonics; each
imposes order upon the material being learned. The first, just
described, is the receptacle mnemonic, in which slots are just
waiting to be filled, and the second type might best be described
as the double transposition mnemonic. The latter begins with
the to-be-remembered material and then makes not just one
transposition upon the material, as in the cases of imagery and

mediation, but two, so that by the time you are finished you have no direct image of the material but only a sort of indirect tie-in.

The oldest and quite possibly the most popular receptable method is one that has been used successfully since the days of the ancient Greeks. It is known as the "house" method. This technique can be used to remember a series of items, ordered or not. It does make use of imagery, but in a slightly different way. In the "house" technique you imagine yourself entering your own house (or apartment) and moving from room to room in the way in which you might ordinarily walk through your house. Before you read any further, actually imagine yourself on this tour. Now that you have this mental map of the layout of your house, we are going to use it as a receptacle into which you place all the items that you may want to remember.

Suppose, for instance, that you were asked to remember these items: elephant, tree, river, automobile, kangaroo, church. Although this list is totally meaningless, you could memorize it (and even in order) by using your "house" method. Ask yourself what the first room is when you enter your house. Say it's the foyer.

In this first room imagine a large elephant standing and greeting you upon your entry. Remember to make the image as bizarre as possible, even to the point of having the elephant crushing plants or other objects that you have in your foyer. Now ask yourself what the next room is. Say it's the living room. Since a tree is the next item on our list, imagine one growing right in the middle of your living room. Spend some time on each image before going on to the next. Do you see the tree in your living room? Then what's your next room? Perhaps it's the bathroom. Imagine a river is flowing through your bathroom (coming out of the toilet perhaps). Now, put an automobile on your bed in your bedroom; imagine a kangaroo in your kitchen (cooking at the stove, with your apron on), and finally put an entire church into your dining room. Now any time that you want to reconstruct what you were supposed to remember (in order), just imagine yourself back outside your house and come in again. What is in your foyer? Do you still see that elephant crushing plants? What is in your living room? Continue walking through your house and see what is in each room. That's all there is to the "house" mnemonic.

The "house" mnemonic can be used to remember some types of information that we've left pretty much untouched so far in this book, for example, what you had planned to talk about during a speech or on the telephone, as well as the order in which you planned to talk about the topics. How many times have you planned to discuss certain things on the telephone with a relative, friend, or client and found after you hung up that you had forgotten to discuss one or two of those topics? Or have you ever forgotten during a speech to a club, or just to another person, what you were going to discuss next? Well, the "house" method will help you to remember everything you wanted to discuss. First choose a key word for each of the topics and then image each of those key words in one of the various rooms of your house. Then as you talk to someone on the phone, or give a speech, imagine yourself going through the house picking up these various topics. For instance, if you were giving a talk on gardening to a club, and you knew that you wanted to discuss: cultivation, watering, pruning, fertilizers, and harvesting, you could imagine your foyer filled with dirt, your living room flooded, a prune in your bathroom, fertilizer in your bed, and an October harvest scene in your kitchen. Now you won't forget to discuss any of these topics during your speech and you'll even get them in the correct order just by making certain that you travel in your mind from one room to the next. As you finish one topic, go to the next room.

The "house" technique can also be used to remember items to get at the grocery store, errands to run, points to make when writing an essay during an exam, things to tell your spouse or date, objects shown during a memory game, or a multitude of other lists of events or objects. You could also use this technique with mental maps other than your house. You could imagine yourself walking to school or driving to work. Along your mental way you would then use distinctive landmarks as receptacles upon which to hang or contain information that you want to remember. To show you just how powerful this technique can be, try right now to remember the list of items that we used at the beginning of this section, not the ones for the talk on gardening, but the totally unrelated items. Use the technique of walking through your house and see what is in each room. Can you still remember all the items that we put in your house? If so, then you are already able to use the technique well and should begin to practice it often.

The second type of mnemonic that we will discuss is a bit more complicated since it makes use of double transpositions. Usually this means that some form of mediation between the actual information that you want to remember to a more meaningful verbal representation is then followed by some form of imagery. For example, we may choose to form words from the first letters of the shopping list: corn, napkins, lettuce, bread, soda, peas (PaLS CaBiN). From these words we could then form an image of our pal's cabin or of our pals in a cabin. To remember the shopping list you could carry an image created from the words that you formed out of the first letters of the items on the list. This way you won't have to keep rehearsing the mediating words because you now have an image to use to remember the mediator. This is why it is called a double transposition: you go from the actual items to a mediator and then to an image. You are now far away from remembering the actual items, but you can still reconstruct them by remembering your image of the mediating word, then using these words to remember the list. It may seem a bit like magic since this is the first time that you have probably heard about this technique, but it has proven to be a highly efficient way to remember information and it can be put to work by you. Try right now to reconstruct the shopping list from your image of the mediator. Easy, right? Now try making up mediators and an image for the mediators for this list (remember you don't have to do them in order): hammer, nails, saw, drill, protractor, level. Do you have a mediator and an image of that mediator? Is it a really good image? We'll find out when you're asked to reconstruct this list of *tools* later in this chapter.

You can probably already see that double transpositions would be useful in helping us to remember numbers. You would translate each digit into its appropriate letter, then form mediating words from the letters, and finally, you would make images out of these words. This mnemonic is really a triple transposition: numbers to letters to words to images. Examples of this system and its application to remembering telephone numbers, license plate numbers, social security numbers, and so on will be given in the section of this chapter that deals specifically with retention of numbers.

One other type of mnemonic should be mentioned before we discuss what specific mnemonics to employ with each of the topics we have been following throughout this book. This last type of mnemonic varies with what you are trying to remember, and therefore it is impossible to give it a general description. However, it would be helpful if you were aware of its existence and usefulness. Basically, it makes use of a poem, jingle, or a rhyme that is more or less imposed upon the information in order to aid your retention of that material. Often this jingle or rhyme has nothing whatsoever to do with the material itself, yet its very imposition upon the material aids in its retention. For instance, the famous poem:

> Thirty days hath September
> April, June, and November . . .

helps you to remember how many days there are in a month even though

> Thirty days hath September
> May, July, and October . . .

rhymes just as well. It's just that the correct jingle "sounds" right when you add the months to it and so it helps you to remember the number of days in each month. In a similar manner most children in our country learn the alphabet through a sort of singsong method that is difficult to describe but is an experience that most of us had in our youth. Ask any five- to seven-year-old to recite the alphabet and you'll find that the child will sing you a song in which "l m n o p" sounds like one continuous letter. But it helped the child to learn the alphabet and it helps the child to remember it whenever she or he wants to.

Advertisers always try to create jingles that will catch our attention and force us to remember their product. The "Pepsi generation" song, Coke's "It's the real thing," TWA's "Up, up and away," and United's "Fly the friendly skies" are all highly successful jingles because they help you remember the soft drink or airline company's name. This author has found the jingle that accompanies the phone number 800–325–3535 to be a very useful mnemonic, but it is not a very good advertisement because the company whose number this is is not included in the jingle. Consequently, I go around singing the number, having no idea to whom it belongs (I wonder if anyone from that company is reading this book).

Now we will turn to the description of mnemonics' application to specific types of information. In some cases the receptacle method will be used, in some the double transposition method, and occasionally the rhyme-jingle technique, though this latter method is rather highly specialized. Incidentally, do you happen to remember the list of tools you were asked to double transpose? If you do, that's great. If not, refresh yourself on it and we'll ask you again later.

### Names

Double transpositions can be used in two ways as aids in your memorization of names and the faces that go with them. The first is to try to make a concrete mediator, or mediators, out of the person's name and then image these mediators. This is easy with names like Harry Stone and Bill White which can be easily, even directly, mediated and imaged. However, you can also use the technique with names like Cleveland (a cleavage in the land),

Forrester (a girl in the forest), Kameron (a camera with the flashbulb on), Pageloni (a long page), and so on. In every case a concrete mediator must first be formed and then imaged. Thereafter, it is the image that you retain, not the mediator. When it comes time to remember the name, you have to be able to reconstruct these mediators from the image and then reconstruct the name from the mediators. All this reconstruction will be quite automatic if the mediators and the image were good ones in the first place.

The second way that double transpositions can be made for names is to make a word out of the initials of the person's name  and then image that word. Of course, this is not as good a system for remembering names as the one just described, but it can be useful whenever it is impossible for you to create a good mediator from a person's name. At least this latter way you can remember the initials, and nine times out of ten that will be sufficient to cue you in to remembering the entire name. The name Charles Pehantousky is a very difficult one to mediate and image. Perhaps you can find a way; if not, perhaps you can  remember his initails C.P. by the word *cop* or *cup*. If you then image that word, the next time you see him you will think of the "cop" and then you can try to remember his name from his initials. It's not as good a system as the one above but it works often enough and it is far better to use that nothing at all. With nothing at all, you are sure to forget. At least with this method you have a fighting chance to remember.

You will remember from the chapter on imagery that it is important in attaching names to faces that you visualize the person's outstanding characteristic (the one you first attended to) and make that visualization a part of your image along with the image you have of the person's name. If Forrester has bushy hair, then imagine that his hair is a forest and that there is a girl (her) lost in there. If Kameron has big eyes, then imagine that each eye is a camera with flashbulbs popping. C.P. should be visualized dressed like a policeman and S.N.W. should be viewed as if his dandruff were snow. This completes the picture then;

not only do we have an image that we can use to reconstruct the person's name, but we have the person's face, body, or outstanding feature as part of our image. That, in a nutshell, represents the most efficient system that you can use to remember names.

Before going on to numbers, let's find out if you still remember the list of tools from the preceding section. How are you doing? Is it working? Keep practicing!

## *Numbers*

The mnemonic device that is used to remember numbers is also a version of the double transposition mnemonic. Basically this procedure involves translating each number into a letter, combining these letters into mediating words (concrete, if possible), and then forming an image of these mediating words. The only thing that has been added to what was discussed in the chapter on mediation of numbers is imagining these numbers. It is the image that we will retain rather than the mediating words. The words can be reconstructed from our image, then the letters can be determined, and finally we can arrive at the original digits of the number. Let's take an example that we used previously in the mediation chapter, namely the telephone number:

254–0830

We transposed this to

n l r s v m z

which became:

NaiLeR SaVe MaZe

Now you should form an image of someone nailing a maze onto a tree in order to save it from a tidal wave. From this image you will be able to reconstruct the letters "n l r s v m z" and then the digits 2 5 4 0 8 3 0, which was the telephone number you originally wanted to memorize.

Try this technique with your own phone number. Translate each number into a letter using our system in which:

$$1 = t$$
$$2 = n$$
$$3 = m$$
$$4 = r$$
$$5 = l$$
$$6 = sh, ch$$
$$7 = k, c, g$$
$$8 = f, v, ph$$
$$9 = p, b, d$$
$$0 = z, s$$

Then form words out of your letters and finally form an image of these words. Now you have a way to always remember your own phone number, which is sometimes difficult because you so rarely call your own number. Try the same system on some of your friends' numbers and then use it for all the numbers that you want to remember. It may not come easy at first, but eventually you will be able to do it quickly, the images you form will be more vivid, and you will also be able to reconstruct the number from the image much more readily. But all this takes practice, so use the technique as often as possible.

You can also use this same technique to memorize your social security number, your license plate number, or dates for people's birthdays; June 24 is 6/24 which transposes to *sh, n, r,* or SHiNeR, so I always remember to give a shiner (black eye) to someone who has a birthday on June 24. This system is by far the best mnemonic to use with numbers, so it is the only one that we will give you to use. Try it out and see how well it works.

### *Lists*

We have already seen that lists of information can be remembered using the "house" receptacle technique. In this section we will introduce a second widely used receptacle technique that has proven to be extremely useful in the memorization of a list of up to ten items. This technique is called the "one is a bun" technique for reasons that will become obvious later. But before you can use this technique there is a little poem that you are going to have to memorize. In this poem you will learn to substitute a concrete word for each of the digits from one to ten. Then whenever you have to memorize a list, you will be able to image each item along with the concrete objects in the poem. This will help you remember the items in the list and help you preserve the order. This mnemonic is a combination of the double transposition and receptacle methods, because first it requires that you transpose the number of each item on the list (is it the first, third, eighth, etc.?) into a word that rhymes with the number. This word is always the same word for each list. Then you have to form an image of this word. Following this double transposition of number to word to image, the specific item on the list is then imaged in combination with the image you have just formed from your double transposition. Spend some time memorizing this poem and you will discover that the mnemonic is one of the very best ways you can use to remember lists.

> One is a bun.
> Two is a shoe.
> Three is a tree.
> Four is a door.
> Five is a hive.
> Six is sticks.
> Seven is heaven.
> Eight is a gate.
> Nine is a line.
> Ten is a hen.

Now, can you form an image for each of these items? Heaven may be a bit difficult, but make up some celestial image with clouds, angels, or whatever. Practice the list by asking yourself what the rhyming word is for each number in order and out of order. For instance what is the word and image for an eight? What is two? What is ten? It may take you ten or fifteen minutes to learn this list, but the time that you spend doing it now will pay off for you in the future. Try to get so that the image pops into your head as soon as you think of the number. Do not go on to the next paragraph until you've mastered this poem.

Okay, now that you know the poem, let's see how it can be used to help you remember lists of even totally unrelated items and in their proper order. Try to form an image of the first item in the list (the number one item) combined with a bun (since one is a bun). For example, let's say the first item is a feather. You should form an image in which the feather is stuck into the bun like a feather in a cap. It's important that the two objects interact with one another in your image, that is, that one is in, on, under, stuck into, or held by the other, rather than just side by side. An interacting image reinforces the fact that the two are supposed to be remembered together. Later, when you are asked what the first item in the list was, you can call forth your image of a bun and then "see" what item was stuck into the bun. Did you immediately see a feather?

To remember the second item in the list you should image that item interacting with your shoe. Say the item is a pipe. Put the pipe in you shoe or put your shoe into the bowl of a very large pipe or have your shoe smoking a pipe. Continue now to the third item in the list and form an image of that item with a tree, the fourth with a door, and so on. Later when someone asks you what the fourth item on your list is, you will be able to remember a door and the item that went with it in your image. So, basically you are using the preformed images from the poem as receptacles into which you are placing the items in any list you want to remember. Let's try it now with a new list of ten items. Remember to form an image of each item interacting with the appropriate image for each number in the poem. Take your time doing it, there is no hurry on this. Here is the list:

1. radio
2. notebook
3. cigarette
4. briefcase
5. chair
6. dish
7. knife
8. chalk
9. book
10. coat

Now that you have formed an image of each item in the list along with its corresponding word in the poem, look at a clock for one minute without thinking of the words. Then look back at this page. Now ask yourself what was number 4? What was number 7? How about 2, then 6, then 10, 8, 1, 9, 3, 5? How many were you able to remember? The average for this list without using the poem is only three out of ten. With the poem it is seven out of ten. How did you fare? With practice you can easily get up to ten out of ten.

The beauty of this poem is that it can be used again and again, always using the same images. In addition, it can be extended to include more than ten items just by doubling up on your images. A bun could be imaged in conjunction with both the number one item and the number 11 item on a list so that you could get a list of twenty memorized. Try this technique next time you play a memory game at a party. It will amaze everyone there when you remember fifteen or twenty items that were displayed on a tray, or can remember a string of items such as animals on Old Macdonald's farm. But, above all, practice using it for everyday lists of items that you want to remember. You can use it for absolutely any list at all.

Remember also that there is more than just one kind of receptacle method for the learning of lists. Don't forget the "house" method. It is the best one to use when you have to remember things in order and aren't going to be able to spew them out 1, 2, 3, 4, 5, but rather have to progress slowly from one item to the next, as in a speech. If you used the "one is a bun" method with a speech you might lose track of which number you are currently speaking about, but in your house you always know what room you are in and which one comes next. In cases where you have to remember all the items at once, the "one is a bun" method probably works best. However, if you find one is more to your liking than the other, and maybe easier and more natural for you, you should use it all the time and not worry about using the other. You will find that if you gain skill with either technique, it will come in handy more times than you might now expect.

### *Everyday Information*

Both the receptacle and the double transposition techniques can be used effectively to aid in the retention of everyday information. The receptacle method is the best one to use to remember lists of information or anything that involves a series, such as instructions or steps that have to be performed in a particular order. The double transposition method is best for remembering paired items, such as what goes with what, who belongs where, or where should you be when. It is also the best method for the retention of single bits of isolated information. Let's take a look at the application of this latter method first because probably we need to use paired-associate memory in our everyday experiences more than we use serial or ordered memory.

Do you sometimes find that you can't remember the names of people who star in certain movies? Do you often end up saying, "You know, what's his name"? If this ever happens to you, you realize that this would be a good instance where a paired-associate might better be remembered using a mnemonic. If movies don't interest you, then you might like to try this technique when you want to remember who sings a particular song, or who conducts a particular orchestra, or who wrote a particular book.

In all these instances you should make a double transposition of the person's initials and image this along with the item to which you want to attach his name. If you can think of a double transposition of the person's name, and this transposition reminds you of the object to which it is to be paired, that would be very useful. However, if the double transposition does not automatically remind you of the other half of the paired-associate, you might find that you will also have to transpose the second item of the pair as well. Then form an interacting image of the two items. At any rate, begin by making a double transposition of the person's name by taking the initial letters of the name, forming a word out of those letters, and then imaging that word. Then, if that word is to be paired with another word formed from initials, make certain that you form an interacting image of the two. Suppose that you wanted to try to remember that *R*obert *R*edford and *P*aul *N*ewman were in the movie called *The Sting.* Transpose these two names into RoaR (as a lion roaring) and PiN (imagine a lion roaring with a large pin in his foot and remember to emphasize the roar and the pin in your image).At the same time that you form your image be certain that the image demonstrates that the pin is *stinging* the lion to make him roar. We don't need to make a transposition of the "sting" part of the association to fit it into the item because it automatically became apart of the image we formed from the double transposition of the two names. Later in this chapter you'll be asked to try to remember who was in *The Sting,* and you'll find this roaring lion with the pin stinging his foot will pop into your mind even before you try to think of the actual names of the two actors. Then from this image you will be able to reconstruct their names. This example of paired-item double transposition should demonstrate to you that you could use the technique any time that you have to remember two things that go together. The example should also have shown you that you can form simultaneous double transpositions (we combined images created from the initials of both Paul Newman's and Robert Redford's names) and that a double transposition can effectively be combined with a direct image (we combined each of these names with a direct image of a sting).

Now let's look at the receptacle method and its use in remembering everyday information. Here you could use either the "house" or the "one is a bun" method, but, regardless which you choose, remember to form vivid images as you progress through a list. Let's suppose that someone asks you to remember to mail the bills, call your mother, repair a faucet, and visit someone at the hospital all this morning. Often when these instructions are given to you all at once it is difficult to remember to do all of them. If you use the "house" method, you could put each instruction into a separate room. You could fill the foyer with bills, put your mother in your living room, have a faucet dripping rivers of water in your bathroom (which may be what is actually happening), and then imagine someone sick in your bedroom with a doctor and nurse attending. If you choose the "one is a bun" method, you could stick your mail in a bun, your mother in a shoe (reminiscent of a child's nursery rhyme), a faucet on a tree, and a door with the word *hospital* written on it or a hospital full of doors. Any time that you have to remember a series of instructions or things to do, you could try to remember them through the use of one of these two receptacle methods.

The main thing that you have to decide whenever you are using a mnemonic is whether the information you are trying to remember involves paired items or a series. If it involves paired information, you should use some type of double transposition; if it involves a series, then use the receptacle technique. Before you go on to the next section, try to remember who starred in *The Sting*. Was our prediction that the image of a roaring lion with a pin in his foot would pop into your head right? Were you then able to reconstruct the two names from the image?

### Textbook Material

The use of mnemonics just described can also be applied to the learning and retention of material from textbooks. Again you must first determine whether the material is of the paired-item or list type. Then apply the double transposition technique to paired-items and the receptacle technique to list information. In addition, the poem or rhyme method can sometimes be quite handy when learning textbook material, for example, memorizing the year that Columbus discovered America:

> In fourteen hundred and ninety-two
> Columbus sailed the ocean blue.

As has been stated previously in this book, the main problem in applying these techniques to the memorization of textbook material is that many teachers, and students as well, seem to attach a sort of stigma to it. It is a widespread belief that mnemonics are just gimmicks that should be avoided in memorizing textbook material and should be considered taboo in the schoolhouse. This notion could not be further from the truth. Mnemonics provide a means whereby the learning of the actual material can progress much more rapidly than learning each item by rote. Just because the system is determined prior to the introduction of what you have to remember does not mean that the system cannot be adapted to use effectively with any type of material. Research has shown that students who use mnemonics learn faster, remember more, and get better grades than students who do not use mnemonics.

Think how much harder it is to learn and remember that $\pi = 3.14$ instead of $\pi = \text{MeTeR}$ ($3 = m$, $1 = t$, $4 = r$). It's much easier to remember the latter. Anyway it really isn't that important how the material is remembered, but rather that it is remembered somehow. Doesn't it make sense then to use the best system of memorizing that is available? Interestingly enough the Greeks and Romans taught mnemonics to their students and they encouraged its application in as many ways as could be imagined. There are stories of Roman senators who could deliver prepared day-long speeches without a single note to aid them through the use of mnemonics. Obviously the ancients didn't have greater mental capacities, they just had a healthier attitude toward the use of memory aids. They didn't view the aids as detracting from the actual information but viewed them as helping in the retention of this information.

It is time that our school systems let all of our students in on these techniques for memorization. Courses on how to improve one's memory should be reintroduced into our curriculums and taught as actual academic courses and not be relegated to the darkest recesses of the school's basement in an area taboo to the students. Students should be encouraged to devise their own systems and should be rewarded when they are successful in memorizing large chunks of material using their system. A lot of students who are turned off by school because it is so structured, mechanical, and uninteresting could be turned on by being allowed to memorize using faster and easier methods. Also their motivation could be maintained on a higher level because they would find themselves progressing faster.

It is also incorrect to assume that students will not be able to use material that is memorized using mnemonics. Why should it be any easier to use the table of chemical elements after it was learned by rote than it would be when a mnemonic aided the learning process? In fact, it would probably be easier to use after learning it mnemonically because retrieval would definitely be faster and more automatic. Furthermore, the student could go on to learning more about the table when the table is well memorized than if he or she kept forgetting certain symbols because they didn't follow directly from the word they symbolize. In the hands of a skilled instructor, the use of mnemonics can greatly accelerate the students' learning progress, can increase their interest in the subject, and can make the course come alive.

We hope you will not be above using mnemonics when studying from a textbook or a manual of instruction. Your classmates, or your fellow employees, will be aghast and amazed at how fast you can memorize the material and how well you are able to remember it. Before you know it, they will be after you to teach them how you do it. The fact that you learn faster and remember better will also accelerate your progress through the required courses in your school or business. But always remember that, like anything else in life, the successful use of these techniques takes practice. You will be able to use them better each time that you apply them to your learning and memorization. Lack of practice will make you rusty. So, even after you've mastered the techniques, brush them off occasionally and give them a little practice.

# seven

# Review

## DOUBLING BACK TO INTEGRATE
## OUR MEMORY

❉ Now THAT you have learned several new techniques designed to improve your memory, it may prove beneficial for you to pause and review what some of these methods are and to place them in their proper perspective. Probably it's advice that you have heard over and over in your lifetime, but it remains an important factor in remembering information. Reviewing information you have learned and memorized actually does more toward maintaining that information in memory than any other thing you could do. This review should include both the basic information that you want to remember and the mediator, image, or mnemonic that you have formed to aid your retention of that information. If you are trying to remember a number by mediation, you should review your mediator as well as the way in which it is to be translated into its numerical representation. If you are trying to remember a list by imagery, then review the image and the list that corresponds to that image on your way to get the items on the list. You should also review it several times while shopping so as not to miss any of the items on the list.

Now let us briefly go over again what has been presented in this text and then see how you might most effectively use what you have learned. We will begin by mentioning again the fact that researchers have discovered that there are various components to our memory system. We actually possess three distinctly different kinds of memory, each one serving a different function, depending upon how long we expect to have to remember certain information. Our immediate memory allows us to retain information just long enough to use it or to respond to it. Then the material is discarded forever, unless we decide that it deserves further examination, in which case immediate memory acts as a sort of filter deciding what should or should not be further processed into our short-term memory system. We can increase our control over immediate memory by concentrating our attention on relevant information in our environment. Several principles on enhancing attention (the first step in the memory process) were described in the chapter on attention and should be reviewed there now that you can see how they fit into the overall schema of memorization. In that chapter, it was demonstrated that attention serves both to focus on the to-be-remembered material and to direct the rest of our information processing (i.e., memory) system. Therefore, it is important to concentrate upon developing your attentional capacities as a first step in improving memory. You really cannot remember material that you pay no attention to when it first appears.

The second type of memory that we described is short-term memory, or, as it is sometimes called, your working memory. Short-term memory stores those items that you want to be able to remember briefly, but which you know you won't have to remember hours, days, weeks, or years from now. We demonstrated that this system was an extremely limited one and that it relied solely upon your continual rehearsal. However, it was also demonstrated that this limited capacity of working memory can be increased if you take the appropriate organizational measures. If the material in short-term memory can be "chunked" by threes, or by category to which the items belong, or by some other system, then the rehearsal of that chunk increases the number of items in memory beyond the seven items that normally are the limit of short-term memory. Furthermore, this organization prepares the material for transference into permanent memory, the so-called long-term memory system.

𝒳 Long-term memory is the retention of material beyond the sixty-second mark toward hours, days, or even years. Long-term memory represents a system of organization that has probably been developed throughout your lifetime. Any new material that you want to remember must be consolidated into this system in such a way that it becomes a part of the organized whole. Thereafter this orderly network can be systematically explored whenever retrieval of a specific memory is desired. Consequently, the better your system of organization, the more probable it will be that you can retrieve something from it. Three techniques to increase your organizational skills and to facilitate consolidation of material into long-term memory were described in the last three chapters. They are: mediation, imagery, and mnemonics.

The first of these techniques, mediation, involves making sense where no sense has previously existed. This goal can be accomplished either by making meaningful words out of single, nonmeaningful bits of information such as someone's name, or by making words out of the initial letters of items on a list, or by stringing words constructed from items on a list into a meaningful sentence, or by transposing numbers into letters and then forming words. These procedures really boil down to an attempt to verbalize everything in as meaningful a fashion as possible and then storing it in memory on the basis of this meaningful translation.

The second technique of organization into long-term memory is imagery. Imagery involves translating information into a mental picture rather than into a meaningful word. Whenever several things have to be learned at once the image is so constructed that all the items can be contained in that image. Recall then involves retrieval of that image followed by a translation of that image back into the information from which it was formed. So, basically, in imagery the organization becomes pictorial rather than verbal.

The final organizational tool is mnemonics, which involves

either combining the techniques of mediation and imagery (the double transposition technique—or the triple in the case of numbers), or combining the items that you want to remember into a pre-established format (the receptacle method), or the creation of a little rhyme or jingle which contains the information that you want to remember. So mnemonics represents the most creative form of organization, one that combines the verbal with the pictorial. It also represents the system that requires the greatest amount of retranslation of the stored representation of information back into the actual material. Nevertheless, it has proven to be most resistant to the effects of interference and, consequently, one of the best procedures for the maintenance of information over extended periods of time.

By now you can certainly see the amazing extent to which our three memory systems depend upon one another. Naturally, short-term memory depends upon immediate memory's ability to detect relevant information and pass it along for further rehearsal. Likewise, long-term memory depends upon short-term memory's ability to keep the information activated long enough for the material to be organized into permanent storage. But it is also interesting that immediate memory is in many ways dependent upon long-term memory because it is likely that what is considered relevant to us at any given moment is relevant only in relation to our past experiences and to other information we already know. Immediate memory is also dependent, in part, on short-term memory because what is being circulated will help us to decide what next to accept or not to accept. Finally, short-term memory is highly dependent upon long-term memory to supply categories into which material can be chunked and to assimilate this material once it is analyzed so as to free working memory for the acceptance of additional material.

This completes our brief review of the topics that have been covered in this book and perhaps it places them into a little better perspective for you. Now the burden of their use is up to you, though we can still extend a bit of advice to you on how to go about using them. We have tried throughout this book to indicate that some techniques may be more applicable to the memorization of certain types of material than are others. For instance, we have pointed out that names are probably best remembered through mediation. Numbers are best remembered through the use of a double transposition mnemonic which converts the number into a word by translating each digit into a letter, creates words from these letters, and then finally an image of this word. We pointed out that many lists might best be remembered by the receptacle ("one is a bun" or "house") method, while other lists are more easily remembered using imagery. The best technique for the memorization of everyday information and textbook material depends upon what you are trying to remember at that moment. By and large, though, mnemonics have proven best in retaining this kind of material. However, an important point to emphasize is that when you find particular techniques that work particularly well, you should use them as often as possible. You certainly cannot be expected to use every technique described in this book. *Nobody* does. If you find particular instances in which your favorite technique doesn't work well (for instance, pure imagery does not work well with numbers), try to combine that technique with some other method to remember the material (numbers can be remembered by imagery but only following a double transposition). The important thing is that you develop your own personal strengths and use them to your advantage when learning and memorizing information of any sort.

Don't, however, try to settle on any one procedure until you have given them all a fair try. Some of them (especially, double transpositions) take longer to learn and are less automatic than others. Consequently, they may require more practice to master, but once mastered they may turn out to be among your favorite techniques. So, if one doesn't work at first, don't get discouraged and discard it immediately; keep trying. You didn't quit trying to learn to read right away simply because it wasn't easy. And now that you can read, you wouldn't want to trade it in for another system of visually conveying information, would you? So go back in this book, review the principles of each technique, and try each one out for a while. It may take you several months or a year to decide which techniques you use most effectively; don't rush it.

Above all else, practice using these techniques even after you've decided upon the one or two particular methods that you most fancy. Practice will make their use more and more automatic, and it will continue to improve your memorizing skills. As we pointed out in the introduction to this book, there are no magic solutions which, once revealed, increase your memory powers all at once. There are, however, many techniques which, once understood, can be used to gradually improve your memory. But, they will do so only if they are used and re-used. Simply knowing how to improve your memory does not improve it. You have to work at improving your memory, just as you have to work to improve any skill. Of course, we must assume that you are willing to practice or else you would not have read this book.

Now that you have completed this book, you have my encouragement to continue practicing and improving, and you have my prediction that you will soon be reaping the benefits of your improved memory.

# Index

f.